Date Due

BRODART, INC.   Cat. No. 23 233   Printed in U.S.A.

ABSTRACTION AND EMPATHY

ABSTRACTION AND EMPATHY

A Contribution
to the Psychology of Style

by

WILHELM WORRINGER

Translated by Michael Bullock

INTERNATIONAL UNIVERSITIES PRESS, INC

New York

Translated from the German

ABSTRAKTION UND EINFÜHLUNG (1908)

First published in the United States of America 1953
Reprinted 1963
Reprinted 1967

Printed in Great Britain

CONTENTS

FOREWORD TO THE NEW IMPRESSION
1948

FORTY years have passed since the genesis of this work. Forty years during which it has proved its continually effective vitality by the incessant need for new editions.

I cannot help being aware of how much the publication of this doctorate thesis of a young and unknown student influenced many personal lives and the spiritual life of a whole era. Far beyond professional and national boundaries. It became an 'Open Sesame' for the formulation of a whole range of questions important to the epoch.

Looking back objectively, I am fully aware that the unusually wide influence exercised by this first work is to be explained by the conjunction, quite unsuspected by myself, of my personal disposition for certain problems with the fact that a whole period was disposed for a radical reorientation of its standards of aesthetic value. Unequivocal proof of the degree to which the times were ripe for such an exposition is provided by the immediacy with which its theories, which were concerned only with historical interpretation, were transposed so as to apply to contemporary movements in the artistic conflict. Thus at the time, without knowing it, I was the medium of the necessities of the period. The compass of my instinct had pointed in a direction inexorably preordained by the dictate of the spirit of the age.

I need hardly say that for me, after four decades of living development, this first work has long since become the object merely of historical reminiscence and evaluation. My attitude toward my old publisher's friendly invitation to place it under discussion once again by to-day's post-war generation, by means of a new edition, is therefore entirely neutral. It is simply as a participant in contemporary history that I await the answer to the question of whether it really still has something to say to the seeker of to-day.

In old age we become contemplative. This explains, and I hope excuses, the need which I feel and to which I shall give way, on the republication of this work of my youth, to enliven the new reader's approach to it by recounting in the tones of personal reminiscence something of the strange events which, in that guise of coincidence so often assumed by necessity, played a part in the story of the genesis and early operation of the essay, and which now form an inseparable element in the memory of my first entry into the field of spiritual endeavour. They confirm the conception of the mediary character of my function as a publicist at that time, at which I arrived later and to which I have already referred.

I will begin. On a visit to Paris for purposes of study, duty leads the young student of art history, whose maturity of development is not yet such as to have presented him with a choice of subject for his thesis, into the Trocadéro Museum. A grey forenoon destitute of all emotional atmosphere. Not a soul in the museum. The solitary sound: my footsteps ringing in the wide halls in which all other life is extinct. Neither does any stimulating force issue from the monuments, cold plaster reproductions of medieval cathedral sculpture. I compel myself to study 'the rendering of drapery'. Nothing more. And my impatient glance is frequently directed toward the clock.

Then . . . an interruption! A door in the background opens, admitting two further visitors. What a surprise as they draw nearer: one of them is known to me! It is the Berlin philosopher, Georg Simmel. I have only a fleeting acquaintance with him dating from semesters at Berlin years ago. During this period I once 'gatecrashed' two of his lectures. For his name was then in the mouths of all my friends with intellectual interests. All that had remained to me from these two hours, since I had not been initiated into his philosophy, was the powerful impression of his spiritual personality, which the manner of his lecturing conveyed with such remarkable clarity.

Well, besides my own steps, those of Simmel and his companion now ring past the monuments. Of their conversation all I can hear is an unintelligible echo.

Why do I relate this situation in such detail? What is so remarkable and memorable about it? This: it was the ensuing hours spent in the halls of the Trocadéro with Simmel, in a contact consisting solely in the atmosphere created by his presence, that produced in a sudden, explosive act of birth the world of ideas which then found its way into my thesis and first brought my name before the public. But this was not enough! My reason for underlining this chance encounter is its truly miraculous sequel. To anticipate its account: Years pass . . . and one day it is Georg Simmel, of all men, who is the first to react, with a spontaneous call, to the surprise afforded him by the chance reading of my trains of thought!

Back to the chronological sequence of events, however. I shall not describe the state of spiritual intoxica-
tion in which those hours of conception left me. Nor
shall I speak of the pangs that accompanied the
subsequent birth of the written word. Suffice it to say
that what I wrote then one day gave me the right to
the title of Doctor!

But what was I to do about the regrettable obliga-
tion, then in force, for dissertations to be printed?
A question of cost! I was helped by the fact that a
brother in the publishing business had at his disposal
a small printing press. At this press the prescribed
number of compulsory copies were now printed and
beyond these a surplus for domestic use, so to speak—
all very cheaply. The copies for 'domestic use' I then
sent at a venture to personalities I supposed likely to
have either a personal or a purely objective interest in,
and understanding of, the essay. One of these copies
reached the poet Paul Ernst. In his case both reasons
for supposing an interest held good: personal, because
I had met him whilst travelling in Italy, and objective,
because I was aware of his well-known work in the
field of art theory.

With the despatch of this copy, the first link was
forged in a very cunningly fortuitous chain of circumstances. What happened? Paul Ernst overlooked the
fact that what he had in front of him was only a
printed thesis, and not a published work for general
distribution. Strongly affected by its contents, he sat
down and wrote a review for the periodical *Kunst und
Künstler* in such terms as inevitably to attract the
greatest possible attention to the run of my ideas.
Booksellers, who immediately received orders for the
book, searched in vain through their lists of new
publications: this new publication was nowhere to be

found. I myself received personal enquiries. They included one from the young Munich publisher Reinhard Piper, who some years previously had published a 'Munich Almanach', in which a literary contribution of mine had appeared. Naturally, this afforded an opportunity to clear up the misunderstanding under which Paul Ernst had written his review; the consequence was an offer from Piper to undertake the publication of the paper.

Does the reader understand why now, when I look back over the intervening forty years, I feel compelled to relate this story at length? That I feel compelled to relate it on the occasion of a new edition, after two world wars, of a paper that has long since become historic and has probably run into more editions than any other doctorate thesis can ever have done? Is it not worthy of mention that this success was due to a pure misunderstanding and hence to a seeming coincidence? And what different road would my whole life have taken without this providential coincidence? For I should never have taken my capabilities seriously enough to embark upon an academic career. Only the rapid success that followed the publication of my first work gave me the necessary courage. Without that misunderstanding this work itself would have led an unregarded existence in the vaults of the University Libraries.

In conclusion, however, I must return to that miracle which, of all those occurrences, made the most enduring impression upon me and to which I referred in anticipation earlier on. It too assumed the guise of coincidence, but the banal trick of a misunderstanding had no share in it.

The reader may recall what that hour in the Trocadéro, with its chance concomitant of a meeting with Simmel, meant to me. He will then have no difficulty in appreciating my excitement and curiosity when, at least two years later (my work was then already in print, but not yet published), I one day hold in my hand a letter bearing the sender's name of Georg Simmel. I rip it open . . . what does it say? This: that a man of Simmel's European reputation addresses me in terms of a spiritual equality which he takes for granted! And what is his message? He takes my breath away with the forcefulness of his recognition and his agreement! The same Georg Simmel who had shared with me the solitude of the Trocadéro Museum in that crucial hour, with no other contact than that of an atmospheric aura unknown to both of us. Now it is he, who was perhaps the secret and unconscious midwife at the birth of my inspiration, who is also the first to react to the paper in which the seed of this hour came to fruition! It was a coincidence that caused him to read my work at such an early stage: Paul Ernst, a close friend of his, had felt an immediate need to share his discovery with him and had sent his copy on to Simmel. The result of this was that Simmel, after reading the book, wrote the exciting letter which had, and was bound to have, upon the unsuspecting young author the effect of establishing a bridge, both mysterious and meaningful, to his happiest hour of conception.

Chance or necessity? I later became closely acquainted with Simmel, and again and again we discussed the enigmatic stage-management with which destiny created between us this link, that must have been prefigured in spiritual space.

I am sacrificing to the god in which I believe most deeply, the *deo ignoto* of chance, if I recall these enigmatic concatenations to-day and if I feel the urge to enable others to experience them in retrospect.

FOREWORD

'Most potent of all is birth, and the beam of light that meets the new-born child . . .'

WILHELM WORRINGER

Halle (Saale), May 1948

FOREWORD TO THE FIRST EDITION

THE following essay was written two years ago—as a dissertation. In the meantime I have naturally outgrown many of the details of my own arguments and should to-day criticise them vigorously. However, my spiritual development has only confirmed my belief in the book's fundamental ideas and I hope to be able, in future works, to place them on a continually improving and more mature foundation.

On its distribution amongst people with artistic and cultural interests the paper met with a highly favourable reception, generally accompanied by a pressing request to make the work available to a wider public, since it dealt with problems which, in a deeper sense, were of topical concern. It is only to-day that, suppressing all my self-critical hesitations, I accede to this request. For the lively attention aroused by the theses formulated here have convinced me of the desirability of placing them under general discussion. From this discussion I hope that much stimulus and much instruction will be derived both by myself and by others. It will certainly contribute greatly to the refining-process which these so important problems are bound to undergo.

I dedicate this preliminary essay, in gratitude and friendship, to Professor A. Weese-Bern, to whose ever-ready understanding I owe so much help and encouragement in my work.

Munich, September 1908   THE AUTHOR

FOREWORD TO THE THIRD EDITION

THE fact that the success of this paper has made a third edition necessary within such a short space of time strengthens me in the consciousness, which has so often consoled me for the insufficiency and merely experimental character of my essay, that in my statement of the problems and my attempt at their solution I have met the unspoken postulate of many who, like myself, have seen through the one-sidedness and European-Classical prejudice of our customary historical conception and valuation of art.

It is this inner topicality of my problem which has given the book an area of resonance that it could not otherwise have hoped for. To this is added the fact that the most recent movement in art has shown my problem to have gained an immediate topicality, not only for art historians, whose concern is with the evaluation of the past, but also for practising artists striving after new goals of expression. Those misconstrued and ridiculed values of the abstract artistic volition, which I sought to rehabilitate through scientific analysis, were simultaneously—not arbitrarily, but from inner developmental necessity—re-established in artistic practice as well. Nothing has given me greater satisfaction and corroboration than the fact that this parallelism has also been spontaneously felt by artists devoting themselves to the new problems of representation.

Apart from a few minor alterations, the work appears in its old shape. Although I felt a strong need to adjust it to my present conceptions, which had meanwhile developed and taken on fresh nuances, I decided, for various reasons, against utilising the occasion of a new impression to bring the essay up to date by revision. Since such a revision would have assumed the proportions of a new book, I should have found myself in conflict with a further work, which has been written in the interim and is now appearing simultaneously with this new edition at the same publishing house. This new work—*Form in Gothic*—is the direct sequel to the present book and is an attempt to apply the questions it raises to that complex of abstract art which is closest to us, namely to the stylistic phenomenon of Gothic. Renewed deduction from the viewpoints propounded in *Abstraction and Empathy*, which for me are decisive, was quite naturally accompanied by expression of the additions and modifications which my view of the problem had meanwhile undergone.

As an appendix to the new edition I have added an essay on *Transcendence and Immanence in Art*, which originally appeared in the *Zeitschrift für Aesthetik und allgemeine Kunstwissenschaft* edited by Professor Dessoir, but which now, for the first time, occupies the position that belongs to it, namely that of direct supplement to *Abstraction and Empathy*.

W. WORRINGER

Bern, November 1910

I
THEORETICAL SECTION

CHAPTER ONE

Abstraction and Empathy

THIS work is intended as a contribution to the aesthetics of the work of art, and especially of the work of art belonging to the domain of the plastic arts. This clearly delimits its field from the aesthetics of natural beauty. A clear delimitation of this kind seems of the utmost importance, although most of the works on aesthetics and art history dealing with problems such as the one before us disregard this delimitation, and unhesitatingly carry the aesthetics of natural beauty over into the aesthetics of artistic beauty.

Our investigations proceed from the presupposition that the work of art, as an autonomous organism, stands beside nature on equal terms and, in its deepest and innermost essence, devoid of any connection with it, in so far as by nature is understood the visible surface of things. Natural beauty is on no account to be regarded as a condition of the work of art, despite the fact that in the course of evolution it seems to have become a valuable element in the work of art, and to some extent indeed positively identical with it.

This presupposition includes within it the inference that the specific laws of art have, in principle, nothing to do with the aesthetics of natural beauty. It is there-

3

fore not a matter of, for example, analysing the conditions under which a landscape appears beautiful, but
of an analysis of the conditions under which the representation of this landscape becomes a work of art.[1]

Modern aesthetics, which has taken the decisive step
from aesthetic objectivism to aesthetic subjectivism,
i.e. which no longer takes the aesthetic as the starting-
point of its investigations, but proceeds from the be-
haviour of the contemplating subject, culminates in
a doctrine that may be characterised by the broad
general name of the theory of empathy. This theory
has been clearly and comprehensively formulated in
the writings of Theodor Lipps. For this reason his aesthetic system will serve, as *pars pro toto*, as the foil to the
following treatise.[2]

For the basic purpose of my essay is to show that
this modern aesthetics, which proceeds from the concept of empathy, is inapplicable to wide tracts of art
history. Its Archimedian point is situated at *one* pole
of human artistic feeling alone. It will only assume
the shape of a comprehensive aesthetic system when it
has united with the lines that lead from the opposite
pole.

We regard as this counter-pole an aesthetics which
proceeds not from man's urge to empathy, but from
his urge to abstraction. Just as the urge to empathy
as a pre-assumption of aesthetic experience finds its
gratification in the beauty of the organic, so the urge
to abstraction finds its beauty in the life-denying
inorganic, in the crystalline or, in general terms, in
all abstract law and necessity.

We shall endeavour to cast light upon the anti-
thetic relation of empathy and abstraction, by first
characterising the concept of empathy in a few broad
strokes.[3]

4

The simplest formula that expresses this kind of aesthetic experience runs: Aesthetic enjoyment is objectified self-enjoyment. To enjoy aesthetically means to enjoy myself in a sensuous object diverse from myself, to empathise myself into it. 'What I empathise into it is quite generally life. And life is energy, inner working, striving and accomplishing. In a word, life is activity. But activity is that in which I experience an expenditure of energy. By its nature, this activity is an activity of the will. It is endeavour or volition in motion.'

Whereas the earlier aesthetics operated with pleasure and unpleasure, Lipps gives to both these sensations the value of tones of sensation only, in the sense that the lighter or darker tone of a colour is not the colour itself, but precisely a tone of the colour. The crucial factor is, therefore, rather the sensation itself, i.e. the inner motion, the inner life, the inner self-activation.

The presupposition of the act of empathy is the general apperceptive activity. 'Every sensuous object, in so far as it exists for me, is always the product of two components, of that which is sensuously given and of my apperceptive activity.'

Each simple line demands apperceptive activity from me, in order that I shall apprehend it as what it is. I have to expand my inner vision till it embraces the whole line; I have inwardly to delimit what I have thus apprehended and extract it, as an entity, from its surroundings. Thus every line already demands of me that inner motion which includes the two impulses: expansion and delimitation. In addition, however, every line, by virtue of its direction and shape, makes all sorts of special demands on me.

'The question now arises: how do I behave toward these demands. There are two possibilities, namely that

5

I say yes or that I say no to any such demand, that I freely exercise the activity demanded of me, or that I resist the demand; that the natural tendencies, inclinations and needs for self-activation within me are in unison with the demand, or that they are not. We always have a need for self-activation. In fact this is the fundamental need of our being. But the self-activation demanded of me by a sensuous object may be so constituted that, precisely by virtue of its constitution, it cannot be performed by me without friction, without inner opposition.

'If I can give myself over to the activity demanded of me without inward opposition, I have a feeling of liberty. And this is a feeling of pleasure. The feeling of pleasure is always a feeling of free self-activation. It is the directly experienced tonality or coloration of the sensation arising out of the activity that appears when the activity proceeds without inner friction. It is the symptom in consciousness of the free unison between the demand for activity and my accomplishment of it.'

In the second case, however, there arises a conflict between my natural striving for self-activation and the one that is demanded of me. And the sensation of conflict is likewise a sensation of unpleasure derived from the object.

The former situation Lipps terms positive empathy, and the second negative empathy.

In that this general apperceptive activity first brings the object into my spiritual possession, this activity belongs to the object. 'The form of an object is always its being-formed by me, by my inner activity. It is a fundamental fact of all psychology, and most certainly of all aesthetics, that a "sensuously given object", precisely understood, is an unreality,

6

something that does not, and cannot, exist. In that it exists for me—and such objects alone come into question—it is permeated by my activity, by my inner life.' This apperception is therefore not random and arbitrary, but necessarily bound up with the object.

Apperceptive activity becomes aesthetic enjoyment in the case of positive empathy, in the case of the unison of my natural tendencies to self-activation with the activity demanded of me by the sensuous object. In relation to the work of art also, it is this positive empathy alone which comes into question. This is the basis of the theory of empathy, in so far as it finds practical application to the work of art. From it result the definitions of the beautiful and the ugly. For example: 'Only in so far as this empathy exists, are forms beautiful. Their beauty is this the ideal freedom with which I live myself out in them. Conversely, form is ugly when I am unable to do this, when I feel myself inwardly unfree, inhibited, subjected to a constraint in the form, or in its contemplation' (Lipps, *Aesthetik*, 247).

This is not the place to follow the system into its wider ramifications. It is sufficient for our purpose to note the point of departure of this kind of aesthetic experience, its psychic presuppositions. For we thereby reach an understanding of the formula which is important to us, which is to serve as a foil to the ensuing treatise, and which we shall therefore repeat here: 'Aesthetic enjoyment is objectified self-enjoyment.'

The aim of the ensuing treatise is to demonstrate that the assumption that this process of empathy has at all times and at all places been the presupposition of artistic creation, cannot be upheld. On the contrary, this theory of empathy leaves us helpless in the face of the artistic creations of many ages and peoples. It is of no assistance to us, for instance, in the understanding of that vast complex of works of art that pass beyond the narrow framework of Graeco-Roman and modern Occidental art. Here we are forced to recognise that quite a different psychic process is involved, which explains the peculiar, and in our assessment purely negative, quality of that style. Before we begin to attempt a definition of this process, a few words must be said concerning certain basic concepts of the science of art, since what follows can only be understood once agreement has been reached on these basic concepts.

Since the florescence of art history took place in the nineteenth century, it was only natural that the theories concerning the genesis of the work of art should have been based on the materialist way of looking at things. It is unnecessary to mention what a healthy and rational effect this attempt to penetrate the essence of art exercised on the speculative aesthetics and aesthetic *bel espritisme* of the eighteenth century. In this manner a valuable foundation was ensured for the young science. A work like Semper's *Stil* remains one of the great acts of art history, which, like every intellectual edifice that has been grandly erected and thoroughly worked out, stands outside the historical valuation of 'correct' or 'incorrect'.

Nevertheless, this book with its materialistic theory of the genesis of the work of art, which penetrated into all circles and which, through several decades right down to our own time, has been tacitly accepted as the presupposition for most art historical investigations, is for us to-day a point of support for hostility to progress and mental laziness. The way to any deeper penetration into the innermost essence of art is barred by the exaggerated valuation placed upon secondary factors.

Moreover, not everyone who bases his approach on Semper possesses Semper's spirit.

There are everywhere signs of a reaction against this jejune and indolent artistic materialism. The most considerable breach in this system is probably that made by the prematurely deceased Viennese scholar Alois Riegl, whose deep-delving and grandly planned work on the Late Roman art industry—to some extent through the difficulty of access to the publication —has unfortunately not received the attention merited by its epoch-making importance.[4]

Riegl was the first to introduce into the method of art historical investigation the concept of 'artistic volition'. By 'absolute artistic volition' is to be understood that latent inner demand which exists *per se*, entirely independent of the object and of the mode of creation, and behaves as will to form. It is the primary factor in all artistic creation and, in its innermost essence, every work of art is simply an objectification of this *a priori* existent absolute artistic volition. The materialistic method, which, as must be expressly emphasised, cannot be altogether identified with Gottfried Semper, but is partly based on a petty misinterpretation of his book, saw in the primitive work of art a product of three factors: utilitarian purpose, raw material, and technics. For it the history of art was, in the last analysis, a history of *ability*. The new approach, on the contrary, regards the history of the evolution of art as a history of *volition*, proceeding from the psychological pre-assumption that ability is only a secondary consequence of volition. The stylistic peculiarities of past epochs are, therefore, not to be explained by lack of ability, but by a differently directed volition. The crucial factor is thus what Riegl terms 'the absolute artistic volition', which is

9

merely modified by the other three factors of utilitarian purpose, raw material, and technics. 'These three factors are no longer given that positive creative role assigned to them by the materialist theory, instead they are assumed to play an inhibiting, negative one: they represent, as it were, the coefficients of friction within the total product' (*Spätrömische Kunstindustrie*).[5]

Most people will fail to understand why such an exclusive significance is given to the concept artistic volition, because they start from the firmly-embedded naïve preconception that artistic volition, i.e. the aim-conscious impulse that precedes the genesis of the work of art, has been the same in all ages, apart from certain variations which are known as stylistic peculiarities, and as far as the plastic arts are concerned has approximation to the natural model as its goal.

All our judgements on the artistic products of the past suffer from this one-sidedness. This we must admit to ourselves. But little is achieved by this admission. For the directives of judgement that render us so biased, have so entered into our flesh and blood from long tradition that here a revaluation of values remains more or less cerebral labour followed only with difficulty by the sensibilities, which, at the first unguarded moment, scurry back into their old, indestructible notions.

The criterion of judgement to which we cling as something axiomatic, is, as I have said, approximation to reality, approximation to organic life itself. Our concepts of style and of aesthetic beauty, which, in theory, declare naturalism to be a subordinate element in the work of art, are in actual fact quite inseparable from the aforesaid criterion of value.[6]

Outside theory, the situation is that we concede to those higher elements, which we vaguely designate with the equivocal word 'style', only a regulative, modifying influence on the reproduction of the truths of organic life.

Any approach to art history that makes a consistent break with this one-sidedness is decried as contrived, as an insult to 'sound common sense'. What else is this sound common sense, however, than the inertia that prevents our spirits from leaving the so narrow and circumscribed orbit of *our* ideas and from recognising the possibility of other presuppositions. Thus we forever see the ages as they appear mirrored in our own spirits.

Before going any further, let us clarify the relation of the imitation of nature to aesthetics. Here it is necessary to be agreed that the impulse to imitation, this elemental need of man, stands outside aesthetics proper and that, in principle, its gratification has nothing to do with art.

Here, however, we must distinguish between the imitation impulse and naturalism as a type of art. They are by no means identical in their physical quality and must be sharply segregated from one another, however difficult this may appear. Any confusion of the two concepts in this connection is fraught with serious consequences. It is in all probability the cause of the mistaken attitude which the majority of educated people have toward art.

The primitive imitation impulse has prevailed at all periods, and its history is a history of manual dexterity, devoid of aesthetic significance. Precisely in the earliest times this impulse was entirely separate from the art impulse proper; it found satisfaction exclusively in the art of the miniature, as for instance in those little idols and symbolic trifles that we know from early epochs of art and that are very often in direct contradiction to the creations in which the pure art impulse of the peoples in question manifested itself. We need only recall how in Egypt, for example, the impulse to imitation and the art impulse went on synchronously but separately next door to each other. Whilst the so-called popular art was producing, with startling realism, such statues as the Scribe or the Village Magistrate, art proper, incorrectly termed 'court art', exhibited an austere style that eschewed all realism. That there can be no question here either of inability or of rigid fixation, but that a particular psychic impulse was here seeking gratification, will be discussed in the further course of my arguments. At all times art proper has satisfied a deep psychic need, but not the pure imitation impulse, the playful delight in copying the natural model. The halo that envelops the concept art, all the reverent devotion it has at all times enjoyed, can be psychologically motivated only by the idea of an art which, having arisen from psychic needs, gratifies psychic needs.

And in this sense alone does the history of art acquire a significance almost equal to that of the history of religion. The formula which Schmarsow takes as the starting-point for his basic concepts, 'Art is a disputation of man with nature', is valid if all metaphysics is also regarded as what, at bottom, it is—as a disputation of man with nature. Then, however, the simple imitation impulse would have as much or as little to do with this impulse to enter into disputation with nature as, on the other hand, the utilisation of natural forces (which is, after all, also a disputation with nature) has to do with the higher psychic impulse to create gods for oneself.

12

The value of a work of art, what we call its beauty, lies, generally speaking, in its power to bestow happiness. The values of this power naturally stand in a causal relation to the psychic needs which they satisfy. Thus the 'absolute artistic volition' is the gauge for the quality of these psychic needs.

No psychology of the need for art—in the terms of our modern standpoint: of the need for style—has yet been written. It would be a history of the feeling about the world and, as such, would stand alongside the history of religion as its equal. By the feeling about the world I mean the psychic state in which, at any given time, mankind found itself in relation to the cosmos, in relation to the phenomena of the external world. This psychic state is disclosed in the quality of psychic needs, i.e. in the constitution of the absolute artistic volition, and bears outward fruit in the work of art, to be exact in the style of the latter, the specific nature of which is simply the specific nature of the psychic needs. Thus the various gradations of the feeling about the world can be gauged from the stylistic evolution of art, as well as from the theogony of the peoples.

Every style represented the maximum bestowal of happiness for the humanity that created it. This must become the supreme dogma of all objective consideration of the history of art. What appears from our standpoint the greatest distortion must have been at the time, for its creator, the highest beauty and the fulfilment of his artistic volition. Thus all valuations made from our standpoint, from the point of view of our modern aesthetics, which passes judgement exclusively in the sense of the Antique or the Renaissance, are from a higher standpoint absurdities and platitudes.

After this necessary diversion, we shall return once

more to the starting-point, namely to the thesis of the limited applicability of the theory of empathy.

The need for empathy can be looked upon as a presupposition of artistic volition only where this artistic volition inclines toward the truths of organic life, that is toward naturalism in the higher sense. The sensation of happiness that is released in us by the reproduction of organically beautiful vitality, what modern man designates beauty, is a gratification of that inner need for self-activation in which Lipps sees the presupposition of the process of empathy. In the forms of the work of art we enjoy ourselves. Aesthetic enjoyment is objectified self-enjoyment. The value of a line, of a form consists for us in the value of the life that it holds for us. It holds its beauty only through our own vital feeling, which, in some mysterious manner, we project into it.

Recollection of the lifeless form of a pyramid or of the suppression of life that is manifested, for instance, in Byzantine mosaics tells us at once that here the need for empathy, which for obvious reasons always tends toward the organic, cannot possibly have determined artistic volition. Indeed, the idea forces itself upon us that here we have an impulse directly opposed to the empathy impulse, which seeks to suppress precisely that in which the need for empathy finds its satisfaction.[7]

This counter-pole to the need for empathy appears to us to be the urge to abstraction. My primary concern in this essay is to analyse this urge and to substantiate the importance it assumes within the evolution of art.

The extent to which the urge to abstraction has determined artistic volition we can gather from actual works of art, on the basis of the arguments put forward in the ensuing pages. We shall then find that the artistic volition of savage peoples, in so far as they possess any at all, then the artistic volition of all primitive epochs of art and, finally, the artistic volition of certain culturally developed Oriental peoples, exhibit this abstract tendency. Thus the urge to abstraction stands at the beginning of every art and in the case of certain peoples at a high level of culture remains the dominant tendency, whereas with the Greeks and other Occidental peoples, for example, it slowly recedes, making way for the urge to empathy. This provisional statement is substantiated in the practical section of the essay.

Now what are the psychic presuppositions for the urge to abstraction? We must seek them in these peoples' feeling about the world, in their psychic attitude toward the cosmos. Whereas the precondition for the urge to empathy is a happy pantheistic relationship of confidence between man and the phenomena of the external world, the urge to abstraction is the outcome of a great inner unrest inspired in man by the phenomena of the outside world; in a religious respect it corresponds to a strongly transcendental tinge to all notions. We might describe this state as an immense spiritual dread of space. When Tibullus says: *primum in mundo fecit deus timor*, this same sensation of fear may also be assumed as the root of artistic creation.

Comparison with the physical dread of open places, a pathological condition to which certain people are prone, will perhaps better explain what we mean by this spiritual dread of space. In popular terms, this physical dread of open places may be explained as a residue from a normal phase of man's development, at which he was not yet able to trust entirely to visual impression as a means of becoming familiar with a space extended before him, but was still dependent upon the assurances of his sense of touch. As soon as man became a biped, and as such solely dependent upon his eyes, a slight feeling of insecurity was inevitably left behind. In the further course of his evolution, however, man freed himself from this primitive fear of extended space by habituation and intellectual reflection.[8]

The situation is similar as regards the spiritual dread of space in relation to the extended, disconnected, bewildering world of phenomena. The rationalistic development of mankind pressed back this instinctive fear conditioned by man's feeling of being lost in the universe. The civilised peoples of the East, whose more profound world-instinct opposed development in a rationalistic direction and who saw in the world nothing but the shimmering veil of Maya, they alone remained conscious of the unfathomable entanglement of all the phenomena of life, and all the intellectual mastery of the world-picture could not deceive them as to this. Their spiritual dread of space, their instinct for the relativity of all that is, did not stand, as with primitive peoples, *before* cognition, but *above* cognition.

Tormented by the entangled inter-relationship and flux of the phenomena of the outer world, such peoples were dominated by an immense need for tranquillity. The happiness they sought from art did not consist in the possibility of projecting themselves into the things of the outer world, of enjoying themselves in them, but in the possibility of taking the individual thing of the external world out of its arbitrariness and seeming fortuitousness, of eternalising it by approximation to abstract forms and, in this manner, of finding a point of tranquillity and a refuge from appearances. Their

16

most powerful urge was, so to speak, to wrest the object of the external world out of its natural context, out of the unending flux of being, to purify it of all its dependence upon life, i.e. of everything about it that was arbitrary, to render it necessary and irrefragable, to approximate it to its *absolute* value. Where they were successful in this, they experienced that happiness and satisfaction which the beauty of organic-vital form affords *us*; indeed, they knew no other beauty, and therefore we may term it their beauty.

In his *Stilfragen* Riegl writes: 'From the standpoint of regularity the geometric style, which is built up strictly according to the supreme laws of symmetry and rhythm, is the most perfect. In our scale of values, however, it occupies the lowest position, and the history of the evolution of the arts also shows this style to have been peculiar to peoples still at a low level of cultural development.'

If we accept this proposition, which admittedly suppresses the role which the geometric style has played amongst peoples of highly developed culture, we are confronted by the following fact: The style most perfect in its regularity, the style of the highest abstraction, most strict in its exclusion of life, is peculiar to the peoples at their most primitive cultural level. A causal connection must therefore exist between primitive culture and the highest, purest regular art-form. And the further proposition may be stated: The less mankind has succeeded, by virtue of its spiritual cognition, in entering into a relation of friendly confidence with the appearance of the outer world, the more forceful is the dynamic that leads to the striving after this highest abstract beauty.

Not that primitive man sought more urgently for regularity in nature, or experienced regularity in it more intensely; just the reverse: it is because he stands so lost and spiritually helpless amidst the things of the external world, because he experiences only obscurity and caprice in the inter-connection and flux of the phenomena of the external world, that the urge is so strong in him to divest the things of the external world of their caprice and obscurity in the world-picture and to impart to them a value of necessity and a value of regularity. To employ an audacious comparison: it is as though the instinct for the 'thing in itself' were most powerful in primitive man. Increasing spiritual mastery of the outside world and habituation to it mean a blunting and dimming of this instinct. Only after the human spirit has passed, in thousands of years of its evolution, along the whole course of rationalistic cognition, does the feeling for the 'thing in itself' re-awaken in it as the final resignation of knowledge. That which was previously instinct is now the ultimate product of cognition. Having slipped down from the pride of knowledge, man is now just as lost and helpless *vis-à-vis* the world-picture as primitive man, once he has recognised that 'this visible world in which we are is the work of Maya, brought forth by magic, a transitory and in itself unsubstantial semblance, comparable to the optical illusion and the dream, of which it is equally false and equally true to say that it is, as that it is not' (Schopenhauer, *Kritik der Kantischen Philosophie*).

This recognition was fruitless, however, because man had become an individual and broken away from the mass. The dynamic force resting in an undifferentiated mass pressed together by a common instinct had alone been able to create from out of itself those forms of the highest abstract beauty. The individual on his own was too weak for such abstraction.

It would be a misconstruction of the psychological preconditions for the genesis of this abstract art form, to say that a craving for regularity led men to reach out for geometric regularity, for that would presuppose a spiritual-intellectual penetration of abstract form, would make it appear the product of reflection and calculation. We have more justification for assuming that what we see here is a purely instinctive creation, that the urge to abstraction created this form for itself with elemental necessity and without the intervention of the intellect. Precisely because intellect had not yet dimmed instinct, the disposition to regularity, which after all is already present in the germ-cell, was able to find the appropriate abstract expression.[9]

These regular abstract forms are, therefore, the only ones and the highest, in which man can rest in the face of the vast confusion of the world-picture. We frequently find the, at first sight, astonishing idea put forward by modern art theoreticians that mathematics is the highest art form; indeed it is significant that it is precisely Romantic theory which, in its artistic programmes, has come to this seemingly paradoxical verdict, which is in such contradiction to the customary nebulous feeling for art. Yet no one will venture to assert that, for instance, Novalis, the foremost champion of this lofty view of mathematics and the originator of the dicta, 'The life of the gods is mathematics', 'Pure mathematics is religion', was not an artist through and through. Only between this verdict and the elemental instinct of primitive man, there lies the same essential difference that we have just seen to exist between primitive humanity's feeling for the 'thing in itself' and philosophic speculation concerning the 'thing in itself'.

Riegl speaks of crystalline beauty, 'which constitutes the first and most eternal law of form in inanimate matter, and comes closest to absolute beauty (material individuality)'.

Now, as I have said, we cannot suppose man to have picked up these laws, namely the laws of abstract regularity, from inanimate matter; it is, rather, an intellectual necessity for us to assume that these laws are also implicitly contained in our own human organisation—though all attempts to advance our knowledge on this point stop short at logical conjectures, such as are touched on in the second chapter of the present work.

We therefore put forward the proposition: The simple line and its development in purely geometrical regularity was bound to offer the greatest possibility of happiness to the man disquieted by the obscurity and entanglement of phenomena. For here the last trace of connection with, and dependence on, life has been effaced, here the highest absolute form, the purest abstraction has been achieved; here is law, here is necessity, while everywhere else the caprice of the organic prevails. But such abstraction does not make use of any natural object as a model. 'The geometric line is distinguished from the natural object precisely by the fact that it does not stand in any natural context. That which constitutes its essence does, of course, pertain to nature. Mechanical forces are natural forces. In the geometric line, however, and in geometrical forms as a whole, they have been taken out of the natural context and the ceaseless flux of the forces of nature, and have become visible on their own' (Lipps, *Aesthetik*, 249).

Naturally, this pure abstraction could never be attained once a factual natural model underlay it. The question is therefore: How did the urge to abstrac-

20

tion behave toward the things of the external world? We have already stressed the fact that it was not the imitation impulse—the history of the imitation impulse is a different thing from the history of art—that compelled the reproduction in art of a natural model. We see therein rather the endeavour to redeem the individual object of the outer world, in so far as it particularly arouses interest, from its combination with, and dependence upon, other things, to tear it away from the course of happening, to render it absolute.

Riegl saw this urge to abstraction as the basis of the artistic volition of the early civilisations: 'The civilised peoples of antiquity descried in external things, on the analogy of what they deemed to be their own human nature (anthropism), material individuals of various sizes, but each one joined together into firmly cohering parts, into an indivisible unity. Their sense-perception showed them things as confused and abscurely intermingled; through the medium of plastic art they picked out single individuals and set them down in their clearly enclosed unity. Thus the plastic art of the whole of antiquity sought as its ultimate goal to render external things in their clear material individuality, and in so doing to respect the sensible appearance of the outward things of nature and to avoid and suppress anything that might cloud and vitiate the directly convincing expression of material individuality' (Riegl, *Spätrömische Kunstindustrie*).

A crucial consequence of this artistic volition was, on the one hand, the approximation of the representation to a plane, and on the other, strict suppression of the representation of space and exclusive rendering of the single form.

The artist was forced to approximate the representation to a plane because three-dimensionality, more than anything else, contradicted the apprehension of the object as a closed material individuality, since perception of three-dimensionality calls for a succession of perceptual elements that have to be combined; in this succession of elements the individuality of the object melts away. On the other hand, dimensions of depth are disclosed only through foreshortening and shadow, so that a vigorous participation of the combinative understanding and of habituation is required for their apprehension. In both cases, therefore, the outcome is a subjective clouding of the objective fact, which the ancient cultural peoples were at pains to avoid.

Suppression of representation of space was dictated by the urge to abstraction through the mere fact that it is precisely space which links things to one another, which imparts to them their relativity in the world-picture, and because space is the one thing it is impossible to individualise. In so far, therefore, as a sensuous object is still dependent upon space, it is unable to appear to us in its closed material individuality. All endeavour was therefore directed toward the single form set free from space.

Let anyone to whom this thesis of man's primal need to free the sensuous object from the unclarity imposed upon it by its three-dimensionality, by means of artistic representation seems contrived and far-fetched, recall that a modern artist, and a sculptor at that, has once more felt this need very strongly. I refer to the following sentences from Hildebrand's *Problem der Form*: 'For it is not the task of sculpture to leave the spectator in the incomplete and uneasy state *vis-à-vis* the three-dimensional or cubic quality of the natural impression, in which he must labour to form a clear visual notion; on the contrary, it consists

22

precisely in furnishing him with this visual notion and thus depriving the cubic of its agonising quality. As long as a sculptural figure makes a primarily cubic impression on the spectator it is still in the initial stage of its artistic configuration; only when it has a flat appearance, although it is cubic, has it acquired artistic form.'

What Hildebrand here calls 'the agonising quality of the cubic' is, in the last analysis, nothing else than a residue of that anguish and disquiet which governed man in relation to the things of the outer world in their obscure inter-relationship and interplay, is nothing else than a last memory of the point of departure of all artistic creation, namely the urge to abstraction.

If we now repeat the formula which we found to be the basis of the aesthetic experience resulting from the urge to empathy: 'Aesthetic enjoyment is objectified self-enjoyment', we at once become conscious of the polar antithesis between these two forms of aesthetic enjoyment. On the one hand the ego as a clouding of the greatness of the work of art, as a curtailment of its capacity for bestowing happiness, on the other the most intimate union between ego and work of art, which receives all its life from the ego alone.

This dualism of aesthetic experience, as characterised by the aforementioned two poles, is—a remark which will serve to conclude this chapter—not a final one. These two poles are only gradations of a common need, which is revealed to us as the deepest and ultimate essence of all aesthetic experience: this is the need for self-alienation.

In the urge to abstraction the intensity of the self-alienative impulse is incomparably greater and more consistent. Here it is not characterised, as in the need for empathy, by an urge to alienate oneself from individual being, but as an urge to seek deliverance from the fortuitousness of humanity as a whole, from the seeming arbitrariness of organic existence in general, in the contemplation of something necessary and irrefragable. Life as such is felt to be a disturbance of aesthetic enjoyment.

The fact that the need for empathy as a point of departure for aesthetic experience also represents, fundamentally, an impulse of self-alienation is all the less likely to dawn upon us the more clearly the formula rings in our ears: 'Aesthetic enjoyment is objectified self-enjoyment.' For this implies that the process of empathy represents a self-affirmation, an affirmation of the general will to activity that is in us. 'We always have a need for self-activation. Indeed this is the basic need of our nature.' In empathising this will to activity into another object, however, we *are* in the other object. We are delivered from our individual being as long as we are absorbed into an external object, an external form, with our inner urge to experience. We feel, as it were, our individuality flow into fixed boundaries, in contrast to the boundless differentiation of the individual consciousness. In this self-objectivation lies a self-alienation. This affirmation of our individual need for activity represents, simultaneously, a curtailment of its illimitable potentialities, a negation of its ununifiable differentiations. We rest with our inner urge to activity within the limits of this objectivation. 'In empathy, therefore, I am not the real I, but am inwardly liberated from the latter, i.e. I am liberated from everything which I am apart from contemplation of the form. I am only this ideal, this contemplating I' (Lipps, *Aesthetik*, 247). Popular usage speaks with striking accuracy of 'losing oneself' in the contemplation of a work of art.

In this sense, therefore, it cannot appear over-bold to attribute all aesthetic enjoyment—and perhaps even every aspect of the human sensation of happiness—to the impulse of self-alienation as its most profound and ultimate essence.

The impulse to self-alienation, which is extended over organic vitality in general, confronts the urge to self-alienation directed solely toward the individual existence, as revealed in the need for empathy, as its polar antithesis. The ensuing chapter will be devoted to a more detailed characterisation of this aesthetic dualism.[10]

CHAPTER TWO

Naturalism and Style

WHEN applied to the product of artistic volition, the two poles of artistic volition, which
we sought to define and whose mutual
frontiers we endeavoured to fix in Chapter One, correspond to the two concepts naturalism and style.

For a start we must agree about the concept of the
word naturalism and keep it clearly apart from the
concept of the imitative. For it is possible for a finished
work of naturalistic art to present to the superficial
view an appearance similar to that of a purely imitative product, although it is diametrically opposed to
the latter in its psychic presuppositions. Naturalism as
a genus of art must, therefore, be sharply distinguished
from pure imitation of a natural model. For here lies
the point of departure for numerous misconceptions in
the modern outlook on art.

Art has to-day become such a confused, complicated
formation, such a differentiated product of hetero-
geneous components, the diversity of which is no
longer taken into account by anyone, that it is impossible to be sufficiently scrupulous in seeking out and
retracing the individual lines, which have been totally
effaced. To many this endeavour seems like concept-
splitting, yet this concept-splitting consists merely in
carefully segregating from one another two lines which

to-day almost coincide, because we know that this parallelism is only apparent, and that each line, if we follow it back through the long process of its evolution, will lead us to a completely different starting-point. Thus a great deal of what is regarded by the general, totally confused, artistic sensibility as of equal value, appears to the purified artistic sensibility as fundamentally disparate. Aesthetics also has still done far too little toward steering us through this confusion of artistic concepts.

This lack of clarity prevails first and foremost in relation to the concept of naturalism or realism. It is not our intention to weigh these two concepts one against the other, but to take them as identical concepts—we have chosen the expression naturalism, because it seems to us more appropriate to the province of the plastic arts than the expression realism, which is reminiscent of literature—and as naturalism in the widest sense, to contrast them with the pure imitation of nature. The statement that naturalism as a genus of art has, in principle, nothing to do with the pure imitation of nature sounds paradoxical, but it will emerge clearly in the course of further examination.

Above all, we must be clear about the fact that the aforementioned confusion of concepts is more than anything else the outcome of our fallacious conception of the Antique and the Renaissance. For we are completely under the spell of these two epochs. Both epochs represent the florescence of naturalism. But in that event, what is naturalism? The answer is: approximation to the organic and the true to life, but not because the artist desired to depict a natural object true to life in its corporeality, not because he desired to give the illusion of a living object, but because the feeling for the beauty of organic form that is true to life had been aroused and because the artist desired to give satisfaction to this feeling, which dominated the absolute artistic volition. It was the happiness of the organically alive, not that of truth to life, which was striven after. These definitions naturally take no account of the contentual element, which is secondary in every artistic representation.

The absolute artistic volition, as it is always most purely manifested in ornament, where the contentual element cannot obscure the fact, thus did not consist —for instance, at the time of the Renaissance—in the wish to copy the things of the outer world or to render their appearance. Its aim was to project the lines and forms of the organically vital, the euphony of its rhythm and its whole inward being, outward in ideal independence and perfection, in order, as it were, to furnish in every creation a theatre for the free, unimpeded activation of one's own sense of life.

The psychic presupposition was, therefore, not the sportive, trite joy in the concordance of the artistic representation with the object itself, but the need to experience felicitation through the mysterious power of organic form, in which one could enjoy more intensely one's own organism. In fact, art was objectified self-enjoyment.[11]

Delight in organic form resulted in its intensive study, and precisely in the Quattrocento the means frequently became its own end. Until the Cinquecento, the mature Classical art, rectified this pardonable error and restored the real to the position of a mere component part and means of art, and not its final objective. It is characteristic of the modern standpoint that amongst our generation it is precisely the transition period of the Quattrocento, with its uncertain groping, its confused and mistaken endeavours, and its frequently obtrusive realism, that enjoys particular esteem, whereas the Classically pure art of the Cinquecento is the object of an admiration which is only tempered by respect and academic culture, but is at bottom cold.

With the Renaissance, the cardinal lines of European man were laid down. All subsequent centuries, in consequence of sharing the same psychic disposition, were bound to see in the Renaissance and in its parallel phenomenon the Antique, a fulfilment, a kind of ultimate goal; this effect was uncomprehendingly attributed, since the artistic instinct simultaneously flagged, to the outward result, not to the inner experience that preceded it. Because a hint was still felt of the powerful effect and nobility of that art, and because this art still employed reality as an artistic means in the loftiest sense, the real inevitably appeared to the later centuries, with their slackened artistic instinct, as the criterion of art; truth to nature and art gradually came to be looked upon as inseparable concepts. Once this fallacious inference had been drawn it was a short step from regarding the real as the aim of art, to looking upon imitation of the real as art. Thus secondary phenomena were looked upon as decisive values and criteria of judgement, and instead of pressing forward to the psychic process which gave birth to those works of art, critics stopped short at their outward appearance and derived from it a mass of incontestable truths which, however, seen from a higher standpoint, are inadequate and unconvincing.

Because things lie so close together here, the confusion which reigns to-day in matters of art is scarcely to be wondered at. Thus there will be a majority ready to raise an objection and point to the artistic sensibility which is mirrored in the whole of Northern Cis-Alpine art, and whose presuppositions are certainly not to be sought where we have sought them, in the Italian Cinquecento and the Antique. But we too desire nothing more than that the effect which emanates from those great formal works of art should be discriminated from the, so to speak, literary effect which constitutes the basic essence of Cis-Alpine art. It is only discrimination, and not disparagement of the one art in the interests of the other, that we are striving after. For everyone accustomed to pay heed to his inner experiences will repudiate the usual effacement of the difference in the character of their effects, and will be inclined to regret the attempt to link together things of such diverse kinds with the great, nebulous word art, and the habit of approaching them all with the same apparatus of artistic terms and epithets of value. As though each one of these utterly disparate forms of artistic expression did not demand its own terminology, which leads to absurdities when applied to the others. Upon any man who possesses a feeling for purity in these questions of inner experience, such conduct on the part of believers in art must seem almost like dishonesty, and it will confirm his suspicion that a great deal of mischief is wrought with the group of letters that spell 'art'.

In other words, discussion must always be confined to an aesthetics of form, and we can speak of aesthetic effect only where inner experience moves within universal aesthetic categories—if we may carry over onto the province of aesthetics this expression of Kant's for *a priori* forms. For only in so far as it appeals to these categories, to these elementary aesthetic feelings, which are common to all men even if variously developed, does the character of necessity and inner regularity adhere to the artistic object; and it is this character alone which justifies us in making a work of art the subject of aesthetic-scientific investigation.

The essence of Cis-Alpine art consists precisely in the fact that it is incapable of expressing what it has to say with purely formal means, but that it degrades these means to bearers of a literary content that lies outside the aesthetic effect, and thereby deprives them of their own specific quality. The work of art no longer speaks a language that is taken in and understood by those clear and constant elementary aesthetic feelings, but appeals to the feelings of aesthetic complication in us, to that quite different complex of psychic experience which changes with every individual and every age and is as illimitable and inapprehensible as the shoreless ocean of individual potentialities. A work of art of this kind can, therefore, no longer be approached aesthetically, but only individually; so that its effect is not communicable, and hence it cannot be dealt with by aesthetic science. This must be stated with all admiration. For it is no disparagement to say of a work of art that it is aesthetically inaccessible. For its human and personal value may lie in this very inaccessibility, whereas the aesthetic is under all circumstances the non-individual. Here, however, we are in no way concerned with the attribution of values, but with the demarcation of boundaries, a process to which thanks are due if the admiration that is purified by this means grows in relation to both phenomena. Of course, the individualistic Northerner, who always has a long way to go to the understanding of form, that negation of the individual, tends conversely to deem the aesthetically accessible inferior and empty—because he does not understand the language of form— to see in it only the inexpressive and schematic, only unjustified curtailment of the individual need for expression; until one day his eyes are opened to the higher existence of form. Then this moves him like a revelation and makes of him an exclusive Classicist, and that with an earnest fervour entirely foreign to the Romance peoples, in whom the instinct for form is innate and therefore taken for granted. There is no need to search for examples of this course of development.

This originally faulty attitude to the aesthetic significance of form has predestined the Northern peoples for all their confusions and misconceptions in matters of art, and has set upon all their theoretical investigations the stamp of unclarity. The major consequence is precisely the confusion of a literary excitation, which can just as well be achieved through the medium of the plastic arts as through words, with an aesthetic effect. Literary excitation can be kindled by matter alone, and therefore bears the character of the arbitrary, the individually dependent and mutable, and may be achieved simply by pure imitation of the always 'interesting' true to life; aesthetic effect, on the other hand, can proceed only from that higher condition of matter which we call form and whose inner essence is regularity, whether this regularity is simple and easily surveyed, or as differentiated as the laws governing the organic, of which we have no more than an inkling.

We have therefore sought to demonstrate the fact that effacement of the fundamental diversity between mere imitation of nature and naturalism in art is consequent upon the fallacious or one-sided interpretation placed by posterity upon the great epochs of the Antique and the Renaissance. Of the two artistic genera, it is naturalism alone—which did indeed reach

32

its zeniths in the Renaissance and the Antique—that pertains to the sphere of pure art, and therefore naturalism alone is accessible to aesthetic evaluation. Its psychic presupposition, as can be clearly understood, is the process of empathy, for which the object nearest to hand is always the cognate organic, i.e. formal processes occur within the work of art which correspond to the natural organic tendencies in man, and permit him, in aesthetic perception, to flow uninhibitedly with his inner feeling of vitality, with his inner need for activity, into the felicitous current of this formal happening. So that, borne along by this inexpressible, inapprehensible movement, he experiences that absence of desire which makes its appearance the moment man—delivered from the differentiation of his individual consciousness—is able to enjoy the unclouded happiness of his purely organic being.

To this concept of naturalism we contrasted the concept style. This word is also highly elastic in its use and meaning. 'For just where concepts are lacking, a word always turns up at the right moment.' In everyday speech, the style of a work of art implies that which lifts the rendering of the natural model into a higher sphere, in other words that trimming which the natural model has to put up with in order to be transposed into the language of art. Everyone means something different by the word, and a collation of the various definitions and usages of the concept style would illustrate clearly the confusion prevailing in matters of art.

Nevertheless, we shall endeavour to give the concept a clear interpretation derived from the facts of the case.

Since we recognise as only secondary the role played by the natural model in the work of art, and assume an absolute artistic volition, which makes itself the master of external things as mere objects to be made use of, as the primary factor in the process that gives birth to the work of art, it stands to reason that we cannot accept the aforesaid popular interpretation of the concept style; since this involves, as the primary and crucial factor, the endeavour to render the natural model. Rather do we regard as the point of departure and the substratum of the whole psychic process, the factor to which, in this definition, only a modifying and regulatory role is ascribed.

Indeed it is our intention, having associated the concept naturalism with the process of empathy, to associate the concept style with the other pole of human artistic experience, namely with the urge to abstraction. The manner in which we conceive of this connection will become intelligible if we try to sketch, in a few lines, the evolution of artistic experience in the shape in which, looked at from the most elevated standpoint, it appears as simply a thousands of years long disputation between these two poles. To forestall objections, it may be remarked that the line of evolution drawn here is an ideal one only, which will be corrected in the second and practical section of the book. For it is not the aim of this work to present a system, but only one of the many cross-sections which have to be combined before we can arrive at an approximately complete picture of the evolution of human artistic activity.

It will be remembered from the expositions of Chapter One that we took as the point of departure for the impulse to artistic creation, as the content of the absolute artistic volition, the urge—in the face of the bewildering and disquieting mutations of the phenomena of the outer world—to create resting-points, opportunities for repose, necessities in the contemplation of which the spirit exhausted by the caprice of perception could halt awhile. This urge was bound to find its first satisfaction in pure geometric abstraction, which, set free from all external connections with the world, represents a felicitation whose mysterious transfiguration emanates not from the observer's intellect, but from the deepest roots of his somato-psychic constitution. Tranquillity and felicitation could make their appearance only when the spectator was confronted by an absolute. In consequence of the most profound inner connection of all living things, this geometrical form is also the morphological law of crystalline-inorganic matter. Fundamentally, however, this connection does not concern us. We may rather conjecture that the creation of geometric abstraction was a pure self-creation out of the preconditions of the human organism, and that its kinship with the laws of crystalline form and, in a wider sense, with the mechanical laws of nature in general, was not known to primitive man, or at all events did not furnish the incentive to creation.

For we have already pointed out in Chapter One that this preference for abstract-geometric form was not a matter of spiritual pleasure, not gratification of the intellect. We repudiated entirely the assumption that a spiritual-intellectual penetration of geometric form was involved in this stage of development. It must rather be assumed here too that every spiritual attitude has its physical significance and that this must be the issue here. A convinced evolutionist might, with all circumspection, seek it in the ultimate affinity between the morphological laws of organic and inorganic nature. He would then erect the ideal postulate that the morphological law of inorganic nature still echoes like a dim memory in our human organism. He would then perhaps also assert further that every differentiation of organised matter, every development of its most primitive form, is accompanied by a tension, by a longing to revert to this most primitive form so to speak, and in corroboration he would point to the corresponding resistance which nature evinces to all differentiation through the fact that the more highly evolved the organism the greater are the pains it experiences in parturition. Thus, in the contemplation of abstract regularity man would be, as it were, delivered from this tension and at rest from his differentiation in the enjoyment of his simplest formula, of his ultimate morphological law. The spirit would then be merely the instrumental provider of these higher relationships.

Whatever attitude one may adopt toward such vague attempts at explanation, which offer several facets to attack, one thing must be admitted, that the characteristic and distinguishing property of geometric abstraction is the necessity which we feel in it, as a result of the presuppositions of our own organism. And it was this necessity which afforded primitive man that felicitation whose dynamic we understand only if we recall the consciousness of perplexity which must have dominated him in face of the multiformity and opacity of the world-picture. In the necessity and irrefragability of geometric abstraction he could find repose. It was seemingly purified of all dependence upon the things of the outer world, as well as from the contemplating subject himself. It was the only absolute form that could be conceived and attained by man.

He could not rest content with this absolute form, however; his next endeavour had to be also to approximate to that absolute value the single thing of the external world which most strongly captured his attention, i.e. to tear it out of the flux of happening, to free it from all contingency and caprice, to raise it up into the realm of the necessary, in a word, to eternalise it. Since it was no longer possible to achieve absolute abstraction once there was an underlying natural model, all fulfilment could be only approximate fulfilment. And the relation between the creator and the natural model was not harmless delight in copying it in its reality, and enjoying the concordance between the rendering and the object, but a conflict between the man and the natural object which he sought to wrest from its temporality and unclarity. This conflict was bound always to end with a victory that was at the same time a defeat. The result achieved always contained a renunciation and a compromise. The content of the evolutionary process of art consists very largely of the fluctuations in this compromise relationship, at least up to the beginning of our modern art, i.e. till the Renaissance.

In his urge to approximate the things of the external world in artistic rendering to their absolute value, to what Riegl calls their closed material individuality, two possibilities offered themselves to man.

The first possibility was to accomplish this closed material individuality by the exclusion of the representation of space and by the exclusion of all subjective adulteration. The second possibility was to deliver the object from its relativity and eternalise it by approximation to abstract crystalline forms. It was, of course, possible to implement both solutions in the one act, and they were so intercalated that it is difficult to make a clearcut division between them, especially as both impulses have, after all, fundamentally the same roots and are expressions of the same will.

The first inference was, therefore, 'to render external things in their clear material individuality and thereby, *vis-à-vis* the sensible appearance of external things in nature, to avoid and suppress everything that might cloud and vitiate the immediately convincing impression of material individuality' (Riegl). It is therefore self-evident that a rendering in the round of the natural model in its three-dimensionality afforded no satisfaction to this artistic volition. This reproduction, in its unclarity to perception and its connection with infinite space, would inevitably leave the spectator in the same anguished state as *vis-à-vis* the natural model. That, furthermore, a purely impressionistic representation, which renders the natural model not in its reality, but in its appearance, was out of the question is also evident; for such a representation would have renounced all rendering of objective fact, and, in its avowed subjectivity, would not have satisfied an urge which, tormented by the capriciousness of appearance, was snatching precisely at the 'thing in itself'. And nothing gives us a more uncertain report of the material individuality and closed unity of a thing than optical perception. Thus a type of representation had to be selected that reproduced the object neither in its three-dimensional corporeality dependent upon space, nor in its sensible appearance.

It is precisely space which, filled with atmospheric air, linking things together and destroying their individual closedness, gives things their temporal value and draws them into the cosmic interplay of phenomena; most important of all in this connection is the fact that space as such is not susceptible of individualisation.[12]

Space is therefore the major enemy of all striving after abstraction, and hence is the first thing to be suppressed in the representation. This postulate is inseparably interlocked with the further postulate of avoiding the third dimension, the dimension of depth, in the representation, because this is the authentic dimension of space. Depth relations are disclosed only by foreshortening and shading; their apprehension therefore calls for habituation and familiarity with the object—familiarity constructs the notion of the object's physical reality experientially from these indications. It is evident that this pressing call for supplementary activity on the part of the spectator, this appeal to subjective experience, was a contradiction of all need for abstraction.

Avoidance of the representation of space and suppression of depth relations led to the same result, i.e. restriction of the representation to extension vertically and horizontally.

'The art of Antiquity, which was directed towards the maximally objective rendering of material individuals, had, in consequence of this, to do all it could to avoid rendering space, as a negation of materiality and individuality. Not that people were already conscious at that time of the fact that space is a mere perceptual form of the human understanding, but because they must have felt themselves instinctively impelled, by the naïve striving for sensible materiality, to the maximum curtailment of spatial appearance. Of the three spatial dimensions in the wider sense, however, the two surface or plane dimensions of height and width are indispensable in order to attain any notion of material individuality whatsoever; hence they were admitted by Antique art from the outset. The dimension of depth does not appear absolutely necessary for this purpose, and since, in addition, it is calculated to cloud the clear impression of material individuality it was, to begin with, as far as possible suppressed by Antique art. Thus the ancient cultural peoples understood the task of plastic art as consisting in setting things as individual material phenomena not in space, but in the plane' (Riegl).[13]

To supplement this definition it must be emphasised that the aim of artistic volition was not to perceive the natural model in its material individuality, which could have been made possible in practice by walking round it and touching it, but to reproduce it, i.e. to gain out of the fragmentary structure and the temporal succession of perceptual moments and their amalgamation, as represented by the purely optical process, a whole for the imagination. It is a question of imagination, not of perception. For only in the reproduction of this closed whole of the imagination could man find an approximate substitute for the absolute material individuality of the thing, which is forever beyond his reach.

Approximation of the representation to the plane is not to be understood as implying that the artist contented himself with the outline, the silhouette, for it would in no wise have been possible to construct an image of closed material individuality out of a silhouette; instead, depth relations had to be transformed, as far as possible, into plane relations.

This was accomplished in the purest form in the well-known distorted drawings of Egyptian art. And it is typical that here, *vis-à-vis* the Egyptians, amongst whom the urge to abstraction, which dominated the whole ancient world, is so blatantly manifest, art historians—although they could not avoid recognising the presence of a totally different constitution of artistic creation—did not allow themselves to be led by this phenomenon to a revision of their conception of the beginnings of art, but, without any attempt at deeper psychological penetration, have been content to dispose of the phenomenon with the designation 'intellectualism of Egyptian art'. Such a designation is utterly misleading. To designate as intellectualism this instinctive urge to abstraction, which accomplished without reflection an achievement that seems to us to-day, because we analyse it on the basis of quite different presuppositions, the product of animadversion, is inadmissible, as we have stressed in another context; especially since this designation contains the judgement that we have before us an artistically inferior phenomenon.

The original tendency of the ancient cultural peoples was therefore, to win from the unclear factors of perception, which is what really imparts to the external thing its relativity, an abstract of the object, capable of forming a whole for the imagination and of affording the spectator the tranquillising consciousness of enjoying the object in the irrefragable necessity of its closed material individuality. This was possible only within the plane, within which the tactile nexus of the representation could be most strictly preserved. 'This plane is not the optical, with which, if we are at any distance from things, the eye deludes us, but the haptic (tactile), which is suggested to us by the perceptions of the sense of touch; for it is upon the certitude of tangible impermeability that, at this stage of development, the conviction of material individuality also depends' (Riegl).

In this theoretical section of the work we are not concerned with investigating the extent to which this urge to abstraction forced itself through in practice—we shall have an opportunity of discussing this in the practical section; here it will be enough rather to establish the fact that there was an *urge to abstraction* and that, as such, it stands in polar antithesis to what we term the urge to empathy.

As the second postulate of the urge to abstraction we specified the need to connect up the rendering of the natural model with the elements of the purest abstraction, namely geometric-crystalline regularity, in order by this means to impress upon it the stamp of eternalisation and wrest it from temporality and arbitrariness. This solution was closer to hand; it bears more of the character of an expedient than of that strict consistency exhibited in the artistic volition analysed previously. It may be stated here, in anticipation, that of all the ancient cultural peoples the Egyptians carried through most intensively the abstract tendency in artistic volition. They satisfied both postulates. They did not rest content with the aforementioned complicated representation of material individuality within the plane through the translation of depth relations into surface relations, but gave to the outline, which expressed the uninterrupted material unity of the object, a particular additional modification.

'Wherever possible, the line was drawn absolutely straight, in response to a marked tendency toward maximum crystalline regularity in the composition; where deviations from the straight were unavoidable they were incorporated in a curve that was as regular as possible. The beauty of these Egyptian works of art rests in the strict proportionality of the parts and in their domination by the unity of undivided and unbroken outlines which, where necessary, were formed into regular curves' (Riegl). Other peoples, with a less unrelenting predisposition to the abstract, were not long in renouncing the consistent rendering of material individuality to this degree; their urge to abstraction was not so intense as to be able to resist the temptation to make concessions to subjective appearance; they therefore soon contented themselves with the second solution, i.e. with amalgamating the representation with elements of geometric-crystalline regularity. This amalgamation may be effected by a variety of methods. To propound the manifold ways in which this amalgamation is carried out in practice is, amongst other things, the task of the second part of this essay. It may proceed in a purely external manner, or it may be mingled with the innermost organism of the work of art, in order to operate from within outward. The latter is the case with all that compositional regularity which has remained until to-day the pre-assumption of the work of art. This discreet and purified kind of amalgamation, however, was able to force its way through only after artistic experience had undergone certain mutations, connected primarily with the strengthening of the urge to empathy.

On the other hand, the striving to impart to things a value of necessity and eternity by the aforementioned means is outwardly documented by the artist's seeking, in the method just depicted in relation to the Egyptians, to suppress every element of the organic by approximating it to pure linear regularity. The artistic process which makes itself felt in this well-known phenomenon is, therefore, the desire at any price to force the natural model into geometrically rigid, crystalline lines, and not, as it has frequently been made out to be, that of causing a fantastic play of lines imperceptibly to give birth to constructs buttressed by natural images. A sharp distinction must be made here between intention and effect. This need for de-organicisation plays an important role precisely in Northern art. That it is only a consequence of the urge to abstraction is immediately evident.

We will recapitulate: The primal artistic impulse has nothing to do with the rendering of nature. It seeks after pure abstraction as the only possibility of re-pose within the confusion and obscurity of the world-picture, and creates out of itself, with instinctive neces-sity, geometric abstraction. It is the consummate ex-pression, and the only expression of which man can conceive, of emancipation from all the contingency and temporality of the world-picture. Then, however, he feels the urge also to wrest the single thing of the outer world, which captures his interest in outstanding measure, from its unclear and bewildering connection with the outer world and thereby out of the course of happening; he wishes to approximate it, in its rendering, to its material individuality, to purify it of whatever it has of life and temporality, to make it as far as possible independent both of the ambient external world and of the subject—the spectator—who desires to enjoy in it not the cognate-organic, but the necessity and regularity in which, with his attachment to life, he can rest as in the abstraction for which he has yearned and which is alone accessible to him. The two solutions we found were the maximally consistent rendering of closed material individuality within the plane and, on the other hand, amalgamation of the representation with the rigid world of the crystalline-geometric. And no one who comprehends them with all their presuppositions can go on speaking, as Wick-hoff does in his foreword to the Vienna Genesis, of the 'charming, childlike stammering of stylisation'.

Now all the factors we have dealt with in the course of these last exegeses, which are all results of the need for abstraction, are to be subsumed by our definition under the concept style and, as such, contrasted with naturalism, which is the outcome of the need for empathy.

For we found the need for empathy and the need for abstraction to be the two poles of human artistic experience, in so far as it is accessible to purely aesthetic evaluation. They are antitheses which, in principle, are mutually exclusive. In actual fact, however, the history of art represents an unceasing disputation between the two tendencies.

Each individual people is naturally, in consequence of its innate structure, predisposed more toward the one or the other side, and the observation of whether the urge to abstraction or the urge to empathy prevails in its art provides us, at the same time, with an important psychological characterisation; to trace the correspondence of this characterisation with the religion and outlook on life of the people in question is a remarkably interesting task.

The illuminating fact emerges that the urge to empathy can become free only where a certain relationship of confidence between man and the external world has developed, as the result of innate disposition, evolution, climatic and other propitious circumstances. Amongst a people with such a predisposition, this sensuous assurance, this complete confidence in the external world, this unproblematic sense of being at home in the world, will lead, in a religious respect, to a naïve anthropomorphic pantheism or polytheism, and in respect of art to a happy, world-revering naturalism.[14] Neither in the former nor in the latter will any need for redemption be disclosed. It is men of this earthly world who find satisfaction in pantheism and naturalism. And just as strong as their faith in the reality of being, will also be their faith in the under-

45

standing, by means of which they take their external bearings in the world-picture. So that this sensualism on the one hand is coupled with a fresh rationalism on the other, with faith in the spirit, as long as it does not speculate, as long as it does not reach out into transcendence. As such a man of the earthly world, in whom sensuousness and intellect move likewise, full of confidence, within the world-picture and dam back all 'dread of space', we may imagine the pure Greek, that is to say, the ideal Greek as we think of him in the narrow margin in which he has finally shaken himself free from all the Oriental elements of his provenance, and has not yet been re-infected by Oriental-transcendental inclinations.

With the Oriental, the profundity of his world-feeling, the instinct for the unfathomableness of being that mocks all intellectual mastery, is greater and human self-consciousness correspondingly smaller. Consequently the keynote of his nature is a need for redemption. As regards religion, this leads him to a sombre-toned religion of transcendence dominated by a dualistic principle; as regards art, it leads to an artistic volition directed entirely toward the abstract. He is unceasingly conscious of the paltriness of rationalistic-sensuous cognition. What could Greek philosophy have to say to such a man of the world beyond? As it advanced toward the East it found itself face to face with a much profounder view of the world, by which it was then in part silently swallowed up, and in part assimilated to the point of unrecognisability. And the same fate befell Greek art with its naturalism. Our European arrogance is amazed to see how little it finally pervaded the Orient, and the extent to which it was finally absorbed by the ancient Oriental tradition.

To anyone coming from the grandeur of Egyptian

monumental art, which almost surpasses our capacity for apprehension, who has felt even a hint of its psychic presuppositions, the marvels of Classical-Antique sculpture will seem in the first instant—before he has rediscovered the other criterion and grown accustomed to this milder, more human atmosphere—like the productions of a more childlike, more innocent humanity, that has remained untouched by the great dread. The word 'beautiful' will suddenly appear to him quite petty and insignificant. And the philosopher who opposes his Aristotelian-scholastic training to the wisdom of the East, and there finds all the laboriously worked out European critique as a self-evident pre-assumption, fares no better. In the latter as in the former case we are left with the impression that the edifice has been erected in Europe on a narrower basis, on smaller pre-suppositions. One is almost inclined to talk about finely worked miniatures. This is naturally not intended to refer to the dimensional size of Oriental works of art, but only to the magnitude of the sensibility that created them.

The arguments sketched out here may suffice to indicate the inter-relationship between the absolute artistic volition and the general *état d'âme*, and to point to the valuable perspectives that open up at this point.

Fluctuations of the *état d'âme* are likewise mirrored, as has been stated, as much in the religious views of a people, as in its artistic volition.

Thus enfeeblement of the world-instinct, modest contentment with an external orientation within the world-picture, is always accompanied by a strengthening of the urge to empathy, which is latently present within every human, and held in check only be the 'dread of space', by the urge to abstraction. Anxiety diminishes, confidence grows, and now, for the first time, the outer world begins to live and it receives all its life from man, who now anthropomorphises all its inner essence, all its inner forces. This sensation of oneself-in-things naturally sharpens the feeling for the inexpressibly beautiful content of organic form, and paths are revealed to artistic volition, the paths of an artistic naturalism, for which the natural model merely serves as a substratum to the will to form that is guided by its feeling for the organic. Now the artist learns 'to apprehend every random form as a theatre within which to experience the joy of moving hither and thither in the company of nameless forces' (Lotze, *Geschichte der Ästhetik*, 75).

It is superfluous to mention an intermediate stage, which will be dealt with in detail when we come to the practical section. This concerns the process, which is of great importance to ornament and the history of architecture, in which the need for empathy abandons the sphere of the organic, that naturally falls to its lot, and takes possession of abstract forms, which are thereby, of course, robbed of their abstract value. This aesthetic mechanism, as Lipps calls it, is very much in evidence precisely in the Northern artistic volition, and it may be said, in anticipation of our remarks in the practical section, that it finds its apotheosis in Gothic.

We will now summarise once more the result of the investigations covered by this chapter, represented by the definition that all those elements of the work of art are to be subsumed under the concept style whose psychic explanation lies in man's need for abstraction, whereas the concept of naturalism embraces all those elements of the work of art which are the outcome of the urge to empathy.

II
PRACTICAL SECTION

CHAPTER THREE

Ornament

IT is of the essence of ornament that in its products
the artistic volition of a people finds its purest and
most unobscured expression. It offers, as it were, a
paradigm from which the specific peculiarities of the
absolute artistic volition can be clearly read off. This
sufficiently underlines its importance to the evolution
of art. It ought to constitute the point of departure
and the fundament of all aesthetic consideration of art,
which should then proceed from the simple to the
complex. Instead, figurative art is one-sidedly pre-
ferred as the so-called higher art, and every clumsily
modelled lump, every playful scribble, as the first
revelations of art, are made the starting-point of art
historical interpretation, although they tell us nothing
like so much about the aesthetic endowment of a
people as its ornament. Here again the bias with which
we invariably approach art solely from the standpoint of the imitation of nature and of the contentual
element is disclosed. The ensuing disquisitions concerning the problems of ornament naturally lay no
claim to completeness; their only aim is, by high-light-
ing this that or the other particularly striking problem,
to sketch the outlines of a more detailed exposition,
such as is not possible within the framework of this essay.

We will turn first to the question of the geometric style. In employing this designation, we are not thinking of the special geometric style of Greek art, but in a general sense of that linear-geometric mode of decoration which plays such a major role in the art of almost all peoples.

According to our conception of the psychic process of the evolution of art, as set out in the theoretical section, the geometric style must have stood at the beginning of all ornament and the other ornamental forms must gradually have developed out of it. This assumption, that the geometric style was the earliest artistic style, is indeed widespread and is recognised as particularly valid for Indo-Germanic art. Nevertheless, the assumption is seemingly contradicted by a number of phenomena. Thus the whole production of the Early Stone Age (as attested by finds in Dordogne, at La Madeleine, Thüngen, etc.) exhibits a decorative style that operates only to a limited extent with linear-geometric forms and, on the contrary, shows a pronounced and disconcerting naturalistic mode of decoration. And what applies to Europe applies, for example, to Egypt. Quite recently works belonging to a prehistoric period of Egypt, that is, to an epoch prior to the First Dynasty, have been found at Kom-el-achmar, which exhibit a similar naturalism. 'A highly primitive, but astonishingly clear pictorial language, which proves the then inhabitants of Egypt to have been at the same level of development as the primitive peoples of Africa' (Springer-Michaelis). There is almost no connection with the later peculiar style of Egyptian drawing; these wall-paintings show rather the same naturalism based on acute, but naïve, observation of nature as the aforementioned Early Stone Age monuments.

Georges Perrot, in his *Histoire de l'art dans l'antiquité*, feels the incompatibility of these phenomena with authentic art; his judgement feels helpless in relation to them and he therefore simply declares them to be outside the framework of his historical exposition. And Riegl remarks in this connection: 'The discoveries in the Aquitanian caves have indeed nothing evidently in common with the development of the arts of antiquity, in so far as our present purview of them extends. We shall discover more historical points of contact with the later Hellenic art in any of the earliest geometrically decorated potsherds than in the best carved handgrips or engraved animal figures from Dordogne.' He states further 'that there exists no adequate ground for the assumption that any of the European and Western Asiatic peoples amongst whom the geometrical vase-style has been found were still at the same barbaric level of culture as the troglodytes of Aquitania'.

We are therefore confronted by a phenomenon which contradicts the historical evolution of art. This contradiction falls away if the concept of art is understood in a manner in which, reasonably, it must be understood. These naturalistic works of the Aquitanian cavedwellers afford us the welcome opportunity of stressing the absurdity that arises through identifying the history of art with the history of the impulse to imitation, i.e. of manual skill in reproducing nature. These creations are pure products of the imitation impulse, of certainty of observation, and therefore pertain to the history of artistic dexterity, if this paradoxical and misleading expression be permitted.

But they have nothing to do with art in the proper meaning of the term, nothing to do with aesthetically

53

accessible art, the evolution of which leads just as logically and consistently to the Egyptian pyramids as to the masterpieces of Phidias. Anyone who looks upon approximation to reality as the criterion of art must regard the cave-dwellers of Aquitania as artistically more advanced than the authors of the Dipylon style. Which proves the whole absurdity of this criterion.

Springer justly compares these productions with the 'artistic achievements' of African natives. Another comparison not far to seek would have been the scribblings of a child. Neither the productions of primitive peoples, however, nor the scribblings of children can, in our opinion, be drawn upon for comparison where authentic art is involved. Only a biased and menial conception of art, which we have already opposed on several occasions in the course of these disquisitions, can take such comparisons for granted; and if even renowned aestheticians one-sidedly account art a mere play-impulse, no one need wonder that such conceptions have entered into the flesh and blood of the public. The fact is overlooked that the majority of primitive peoples—who, moreover, seen from the standpoint of contemporary science, are not peoples in their infancy, but a rudimentary remnant of the human race left over from long gone by periods of culture and incapable of development—despite their vaunted naturalism, can show no authentic artistic aptitude and hence no artistic evolution either. The eminent artistic gifts of a few particular primitive peoples, which have been exercised in a purely ornamental field, have naturally been passed over by the view of art history that is directed solely toward the naturalistic and have only very recently received the appraisal they merit. A great service has been rendered to this gradual purification of our art historical vision by the discovery of such an exceptionally artistic phenomenon as Japanese art. The study of Japanese art in Europe must be accounted one of the most important stages in the history of the gradual rehabilitation of art as a purely formal organism, i.e. one that appeals to our elementary aesthetic feelings. And on the other hand it saves us from the danger, which lies close to us, of seeing the possibilities of pure form only within the Classical canon.

The scribblings of a child are also not accessible to aesthetic evaluation; the authentic art impulse does not make its appearance until later, and then it admittedly utilises for its own ends the capacity for reproducing nature which has developed in the interim. To regard the scribblings of a child, however acute the observation upon which they rest and however skilful they may be, as artistic productions contradicts a more elevated conception, which considers as art only that which, the outcome of psychic needs, satisfies psychic needs.

Thus, then, the aforementioned products of the prehistoric ages of Europe and Egypt are certainly interesting from the point of view of the history of culture, and are of particular value as regards their contents, but to include them in the history of art would be an error, from which Perrot and Riegl, though admittedly for other reasons, also recoil. The thesis that the geometric style of art was the earliest is, therefore, in no way shaken by these relics. For wherever else we succeed in catching a glimpse of the artistic beginings of those peoples which can show an artistic development, we find the assumption corroborated that art does not begin with naturalistic constructs, but with ornamental-abstract ones. The first beginnings of aesthetic need press toward the linear-organic, which shuns all empathy.

The historical education of our era resulted in an approach in which an artistic phenomenon was never explained in terms of itself, but always in terms of other phenomena. Thus it became the cardinal object of the study of art history to ascertain at all points the influences which were at work. The local starting-point of any artistic phenomenon was established and then the path along which it spread was investigated. Thus the validity of a universal spontaneous genesis of the geometric style was not accepted; the attempt was made to trace it back to a few centres, if not to one single centre of origin. Contrary to the rest of his views concerning the psychic-artistic preconditions for the genesis of a style, we find Riegl himself taking sides with those who dispute the spontaneous genesis of the geometric style. This inconsistency of Riegl's is only to be explained by supposing that it is his intention, by demonstrating the operation of historical influence and diffusion in the geometric style, to campaign against his major foes, the artistic materialists. For the latters' theory led logically to the assumption that the same ornamental style was bound to come into being everywhere, without mutual influence, merely through the existence of the same technological preconditions. And because the theorem of the spontaneous genesis of the geometric style is one of the main arguments of the artistic materialists, Riegl's critique is directed against this thesis with all the fervour he can muster. Little as we are able to feel convinced by this critique that the geometric style spread over the ancient world from one place of origin, we are grateful to Riegl for proving historically, in his controversy with the Semperians, how quickly the thesis of a technologico-mechanical causation of styles breaks down in the face of historical research and how much rather the artistic monuments that really have been historically established tend to contradict this assumption.

From the point of view of our theory, which aims at whittling down to an ineluctable minimum the customary method of tracing historical influences, the thesis of the universal spontaneous genesis of the geometric style is illuminating and a veritable intellectual necessity. The artistic needs of a people must have led it to linear-inorganic abstraction not in causal conjunction with its current technology and methods of production, but in association with its current psychic state. In comparison with these major psychic factors any influences that may have been at work are of only secondary significance.

How does the genesis of plant ornament fit into the line of development which we have hypothetically established? Up to now art historians have contented themselves with two solutions. They have either taken the sudden irruption of vegetal elements into ornament as a result of the imitative tendency, or they have pointed to the symbolic value of the various motifs. The first solution, with its menial conception of the genesis of an artistic form, must be reduced to a minimum at the outset. The idea that any old plant could suddenly have been chosen as the basis of a decorative motif, simply because its specific character was pleasing—an idea which unfortunately comes very easily to us to-day, because of our contemporary artistic laxity—is entirely contradictory to the Antique artistic sensibility. Riegl too opposes such a notion: 'It is an empirical principle derived precisely from the examination of plant ornament as a whole, that the

realistic representation of flowers for decorative purposes, so much in vogue to-day, belongs to the modern
period alone.' And then Riegl continues, in order
to define the character of Antique plant ornament:
'The naïve artistic sense of earlier periods of art
demanded, first and foremost, the observance of symmetry, even in the reproduction of natural creatures.
In the representation of man and animals restriction
was thrown overboard at an early stage, and recourse
was had to arranging them in the heraldic style and
the like; such a seemingly lifeless thing as the plant, on
the other hand, continued in the most mature styles of
past centuries to be symmetrised, stylised—especially
in so far as the plant image was not assigned an
objective significance, but in fact intended as a mere
ornament.' How little Riegl has grasped the salient
point of the process in these statements from his
Stilfragen—which in other respects as well bears a
compromise character *vis-à-vis* the standpoint he
adopts in his *Spätrömische Kunstindustrie*—can be seen
from the fact that symmetrisation and stylisation goes
much further in Egyptian plant ornament, the
objective significance of which is beyond question,
than it does in Greek plant ornament, where objective
significance falls away almost entirely. These statements of Riegl's are also a contradiction of a subsequent passage in *Stilfragen*, where he proves that,
for example, the appearance of the earliest acanthus
motifs lack precisely the characteristic peculiarities of
the acanthus plant, and that it is not until much later
that they can properly claim the designation acanthus,
at a time when the further development of this ornament really did lead to its resembling the appearance
of the plant named. And he very appositely adds:
'Strangely enough, no one has so far been struck by

58

the improbability of the process by which the first weed the artist came across was supposed suddenly to have been elevated to an artistic motif.'

The second solution pointed to the symbolic value of the individual motif. Here the matter is more difficult. For in ancient Oriental, and especially Egyptian art the symbolic value of the motif plays a great role. This incontestable fact must not, however, mislead us into extending its significance over the whole evolution of plant ornament. On the one hand, as already stated, precisely amongst. the Egyptians the symbolic value of the motif vanishes beneath the higher will to form, and on the other, if this inner connection between ornament and symbol really had existed within the whole sphere of culture, it would be incomprehensible that the individual people should not have put up a much more vigorous resistance to the adoption of a particular motif, and the world-dominion of certain motifs would be totally inexplicable. We must therefore rest content with accepting the symbolic value of certain motifs as a *momentum agens* for the genesis of particular plant ornaments—a *momentum agens* that is worthy of our attention, but only on the way to one that is higher and more universally valid.

The greatest psychological probability is possessed, in our view, by the following notion, which arises logically out of our theory. It was not the vegetal organism itself, but its structural law, that man carried over into art. We will elucidate this notion by an extreme example.

Just as the geometric style gives the structural law of inanimate matter, but not matter itself in its outward appearance, so vegetal ornament originally gave not the plant itself, but the regularity of its outward structure. Thus both ornamental styles are actually devoid of a natural model, notwithstanding the fact that their elements are to be found in nature. In the former case inorganic-crystalline regularity is employed as an artistic motif, in the latter organic regularity, which is most purely and perceptibly disclosed to us in the structure of plants. All the elements of organic structure there are: regularity, arrangement round a centre, balance between centrifugal and centripetal forces (i.e. circular curvature), equilibrium between carrying and burdening factors, proportionality of relationships, and all the rest of the wonders that strike us when we examine closely the organism of a plant—they it is which now make up the content and the living value of the ornamental work of art; and only a later epoch approximates this ornamental style, which has almost as little to do with natural models in principle as the geometric style, to naturalism. The process therefore consists in the subsequent naturalisation of a pure ornament, i.e. an abstract form, and not in the subsequent stylisation of a natural object. The crucial factor is contained in this antithesis. For it reveals that the primary element is not the natural model, but the law abstracted from it. It was therefore the artistic projection of the regularity of organic structure which, in consequence of the intimate organic connection between all living things, afforded the basis for the aesthetic experience of the spectator, and not concordance with the natural model.

Both styles, linear as well as vegetal ornament, thus represent at bottom an abstraction, and their diversity is, in this sense, really only one of degree; just as, in the eyes of a monist, organic regularity, in the last analysis, differs only in degree from that of the inorganic-crystalline. We are concerned only with the value this difference of degree possesses in relation to the problem of empathy or abstraction. It then becomes immediately evident that organic regularity, even when represented in the abstract, has a milder effect upon us and is more closely bound up with our own vital sensations. It makes a stronger appeal to the activation of these vital sensations of ours, and is thus calculated gently and gradually to entice out man's latent impulse to empathy.

Observation of the evolution of Northern animal ornament leads to similar conclusions. Sophus Müller, in his detailed investigations in this domain, reached the conviction that these animal motifs developed along purely ornamental-linear paths, i.e. without a natural model, and that, for instance, the designation dragon or serpent coils is entirely misleading, in as much as there was originally no thought of rendering any natural model. He repudiates equally energetically the symbolic character of the motifs in question. 'If according to this theory we were to assume that the whole movement was supported from outside by an exact acquaintance with certain forms of animal, domestic animals, sacred animals, sacrificial animals, ordinary beasts of the chase, or with creatures of the imagination, it would be difficult to refute it along archaeological channels. On the other hand, however, this assumption would find no support in all the accumulated material of archaeology. Of course, the genesis of ornamental animal images cannot be imagined without a general notion of animals, but the ornament affords no grounds for the conjecture that it was intended to portray this that or the other animal' (Sophus Müller, *Tierornamentik im Norden*. Translated from the Danish by Westorf, Hamburg, 1881).

The same applies to the animal ornament of almost all other styles; we have only to look at Graeco-Roman decorative art, Arabian, or that of the Middle Ages. In every case it is not the natural model that is reproduced, but certain structural peculiarities of animals, e.g. the relationship of the eyes to the muzzle or beak, or the relationship of the head to the trunk or that of the wings to the body, etc. With these relationships, these peculiarities of animal structure, the artist enriched his vocabulary of linear forms. That recollection of the natural model was no longer directly operative in this process is best proved by the fact that diverse motifs abstracted from various animals were combined without the slightest hesitation. It was only the later naturalisation that subsequently turned these constructs into the well-known fabulous beasts which emerge in all branches of ornamental art. At bottom these are not the offspring of imagination and they did not exist at all in the fancy of the peoples in question; they are purely the product of linear-abstract tendencies. Hence we have here once again the same phenomenon as with plant ornament. Here too there can be no question of the stylisation of a natural model; here too an abstract-linear construct is gradually naturalised. Thus the point of departure of the artistic process is linear abstraction, which, although it bears a certain relationship to the natural model, has nothing to do with any imitation impulse. Rather does the whole process take place within the abstract limits in which alone both primitive man and the man of early Antiquity were able to exercise their artistic talents. The attempt was made in the first part of this essay to demonstrate the psychic roots by which this unconditional inclination to the dead inorganic line, to the abstraction of life and to regularity is to be explained. From this we shall immediately understand the connection between the process of naturalisation and the need for empathy, which was becoming free.

The anthropologists have recently taken a lively part in investigations into ornament. This is particularly true as regards the primitive ornament of savage tribes. The hypotheses concerning the genesis of linear-geometric ornament put forward from anthropological quarters do not go particularly deep. Thus in part any direct inclination of man to geometric form has been denied and the genesis of the latter in ornament explained by entirely fortuitous factors. For example, we may recall that von den Steinen ascribed the predilection of Brasilian Indians for the triangle to the circumstance that the cloth worn by the women to cover their nakedness is triangular in shape. The proof is simple. The fact that, when a triangle is drawn for them, the men grin and pronounce the word *huluri* is sufficient for the investigator to conclude that this triangular rag is the fortuitous cause of the genesis of a geometric ornamental motif. To pay heed to psychic values in matters of art is as far removed from the anthropologists as it is from the materialists. Von den Steinen goes so far, for instance, as to explain the simple + cross as the simplified linear likeness of a flying stork, an assertion which he supports by comparative photographs.

The validity of such methods of investigation as these, which have been employed by anthropologists with great skill and results which are at first sight so startling, cannot be tested within the framework of this essay nor in the absence of the practical experience which is so richly available to the aforesaid investigators. We must rest content with rejecting them in principle. And let anyone who has allowed himself to be one-sidedly convinced by these theories and their findings, cast a quick glance at the Dipylon style, which all investigators recognise as an evolved and refined style and in relation to which all attempts at an explanation on the lines of the anthropologists with their flying storks and triangular *cache-sexe* would rapidly lead *ad absurdum*. Analogies with primitive peoples should in any case be pursued with the greatest caution. For the measure of artistic aptitude, with which alone we are concerned here and which has nothing to do with the manual dexterity involved in making a lump of clay or a piece of wood look like a man, is so unequal in the various peoples—many indeed showing hardly any trace of it—that all generalisation based on the evidence available leads us into false paths.

Since we are now reverting to a consideration of the geometric style, we must spend a moment considering the concepts regularity and uniformity.* Attempts have been made to discriminate between these two concepts. Thus Wölfflin in his *Prolegomena* is of the opinion that 'uniformity' of succession must be distinguished from the 'regularity' of a line or figure. The difference between uniformity and regularity is supposed to be rooted in a profound divergence of meaning. 'The latter represents a purely intellectual relationship, the former a physical. The regularity expressed in a square has no connection with our organism, it does not please us as an agreeable existen-

---

* *Translator's Note.*—Here and throughout the book 'regularity' translates the German word *Gesetzmässigkeit*; but it is equally the normal translation of *Regelmässigkeit*, which is here contrasted with *Gesetzmässigkeit*. For the sake of this contrast 'uniformity' is used here to translate *Regelmässigkeit*, a makeshift solution which indicates the difficulty of sustaining the verbal distinction in English.

tial form, it is not a universal precondition of organic life, but merely an instance favoured by our intellect. Uniformity of sequence, by contrast, is something we value because our organism, by virtue of its biological scaffolding, demands uniformity in its functions. We breathe uniformly, every continuous activity is carried out in a periodic sequence.'

Schmarsow has already quite rightly opposed to this conception the fact, which Wölfflin himself documents in another passage, that every intellectual relationship has a physical significance as well. Also it would never be possible to explain with this assumption—that geometrical regularity is merely a phenomenon favoured by our intellects—the world dominion of the geometric style precisely in primitive cultures. Rather do we share with Lipps the view 'that geometrically uniform (*regelmässig*) figures are an object of pleasure because the apprehension of them, as of a whole, is natural to the soul, or because it is, to a particularly great extent, in conformity with a propensity in the nature or essence of the soul'.

Nevertheless, the discrimination Wölfflin is trying to make does correspond to a very subtle difference. It may be cautiously hinted that regularity is indissolubly bound up with the impulse to abstraction, whereas the subordinate phenomenon of uniformity already constitutes an imperceptible transition to the province of possibilities of empathy. In a similar sense Schmarsow states: 'Uniformity is the contribution of the subject, regularity is the contribution of the external world, the effect of natural forces.' This does not mean, however, that every instance of uniformity of succession already appeals to the empathy impulse, or rather owes its genesis to this impulse. This empathy value of uniform succession is initially, e.g. in the gcometric style, latent and becomes conscious only in the course of development. This process of the slow entry into consciousness of the possibility of empathy is perhaps outwardly documented by the stressing of uniformity of succession by connecting lines and the impregnation of these lines with expression as it were. With the word expression the situation is clarified. For regularity contains no element of expression *a priori*, whereas uniformity does. As stated, however, this expression only becomes manifest through the language of connecting lines. In this manner the mature geometric style achieves a miraculous equipoise between the elements of abstraction and of empathy. Forms like the Vitruvian scroll and the spiral, as developed by the Greeks, are the highpoints of this endeavour. Particularly the Vitruvian scroll which, in contradistinction to the spiral, dispenses with all affinity to organic forms, exhibits the astonishing process by which the need for empathy takes possession of the rigidly linear, inert line and imparts to it a movement, a life of such intensity and balance as would seem to be reserved for organic motion.

Here we have already referred in passing to the highpoints of Greek ornament, and an analysis of the special peculiarity of the Greek artistic volition is now incumbent upon us. Such an analysis demands a return into the distant past. The way may be prepared for it by a comparison of Mycenean with Egyptian ornament. The *novum* of Mycenean ornament, as is well-known, is the emergence of vegetal motifs. The other components of Mycenean ornament, the Oriental and the linear-geometric, were already contained in embryo in the ornamental art of Hissarlik. This emergence of the plant motif in Greek ornament has also been attributed to Egyptian influence. Without

66

passing a negative judgement on this question, we will investigate the purely formal difference between Egyptian and Mycenean plant ornament. Here too we shall of course approach the problem from the twin viewpoints of stylisation and naturalism, with their pre-assumptions need for abstraction and need for empathy. The comparison is all the more instructive as certain circumstances threaten to veil the facts. According to our definition we should expect Egyptian ornament to bear a purely linear-abstract stamp and, like the Dipylon style, to avoid as far as possible all round, sinuous lines as a transition to the organic. For we are apt more readily to associate the dead, straight, uncurved line with the concept of the in-organic than the curved line, for the simple reason that the sinuous line has a far stronger appeal to our need for empathy than the straight line. Now the fact that the apparently organic-sinuous line plays such a leading role in Egyptian ornament is not due to the Egyptians having taken the urge to empathy as the point of departure for their artistic volition, but to the objective significance of the motifs, which pointed the way to their ornamental art. For the symbolic value of the various motifs, such as the papyrus and lotus, is beyond question (Goodyear, *The grammar of the lotus, a new history of classic ornament as a development of sun worship*. London, 1891). This bondage to the objective, in this case to an organically rounded model, was naturally an obstacle to the evolution of purely linear-geometric ornament. But a glance at Mycenean and later Greek plant ornament shows us how the organic was subjugated by an artistic volition directed toward the abstract in Egyptian ornament. In so far as the objective element was unavoidably necessary, it was translated into geometrically regular, life-alien curves, so that no idea of an underlying natural model enters the mind of the outside observer. The balance between the objective-conditional and abstraction is complete. And so this ornamental style, despite its originally organic basis, gives an impression that is more rigid and foreign to life than any other style. That which, to begin with, disturbs this impression, the predominance of sinuous lines, appears on the one hand as extraneously motivated, while on the other these curves are so regular and so uniform that we are bound to assume that the Egyptian was unaware of their empathy value, that, rather, he enjoyed them as pure geometrical abstraction. The Egyptian, we must infer, saw for example in the circle not the living line that pursues this its predetermined path in a marvellous conflict and balance between centrifugal and centripetal forces and must return to itself, but saw in it only the geometric form which presents itself as the most perfect of all such forms through the fact that it is the only one to fulfil in all directions and *in toto* the postulate of symmetry.

The further development which plant ornament underwent in Greek art lay from the start outside the artistic volition of the Egyptians, and it is erroneous to take this as a reason for affirming, as Riegl does, that the Egyptians' capacity for ornamental achievement was exhausted. Rather is the fundamental proposition valid here too, that what is achieved represents the fulfilment of what was desired, and in so far as the volition does not alter—and in the rigid direction of the Egyptians this remained unchanged—it is also incapable of development.

An analysis of Mycenean plant ornament must set out from quite different presuppositions. Riegl, who considers Mycenean plant ornament to be also

68

a loan from the Egyptian, characterises the difference in the following words: 'The underlying tendency of the Mycenean artist can be judged only by its effect; if the latter was intentional the goal was an enlivening, a mobilisation of the typical stiffly stylised Egyptian motifs.' This naturalising tendency goes very far with the Mycenean artists, in some places even, as in the drawing in of the ribs of leaves, farther than later Greek ornament ever went. Altogether, the naturalism that dominates the whole of Mycenean art shows a complexion which has often been termed barbaric. At all events, it recalls the naturalism of primitive peoples. It thus becomes very difficult to evaluate Mycenean ornament; in fact it is questionable whether it can be included in the authentic artistic course of development of Greek ornament, or whether it must not rather be regarded as an unrelated individual phenomenon. Especially since the geometric Dipylon style stands between it and Classic Greek ornament. Before we proceed to a consideration of Classic Greek ornament, we must clarify our views on the character of this Dipylon style. This geometric style exhibits a maturity, indeed a sophistication, which clearly differentiates it from the geometric style as a whole. Abstraction into the linear is carried out with total consistency. Conze, who has devoted much effort to the analysis of the Dipylon style and, above all, was the first to see in it a high level of artistic attainment, says: 'So far the forms lack any element which could be traced back to the imitation of natural objects. This latter is added when we come to the animal figures; with them the greatest decorative richness of this style has been attained. These depictions of animals, however, are completely assimilated to the rest of the forms made up of the interplay of lines;

they are themselves dissolved into a linear schema, and even on those occasions where the body is blocked in with a fuller brush this linear schematisation appears in the extremities, particularly the feet, in a very uniformly repeated fashion. Here too then there is no uncertain experimenting in the representation, but a quite definite manner that has been found convenient and appropriate' (Conze, *Zur Geschichte der Anfänge der griechischen Kunst.* Report of the meeting of the Royal Academy of Sciences, 64, 1870).

Conze therefore clearly recognises that here, in the seemingly clumsy and unnatural drawing of natural models, it is not a question of lack of ability or of simplification, as for instance in the scribblings of a child, but of a consistently executed stylistic intention that is capable of doing what it wishes to do. And this volition is precisely a purely abstract one, which looks upon every approximation to the organic as a clouding of this desired abstraction.

A more pronounced antithesis than that between the naturalism of the Mycenean style and the essentially abstract character of the ensuing Dipylon style cannot be imagined. And the phenomenon temporally subsequent to the latter is Classic ornament. The question perforce arises as to whether the roots of Classic art are to be looked for in the Mycenean or the Dipylon style. This question is a wide battle-ground. Riegl's standpoint, for instance, is favourable to the Mycenean style. He opines: 'Mycenean art appears to us as the immediate forerunner of the Hellenic art of the luminous historical period. The Dipylon and whatever else lay between was merely an obfuscation, a disturbance of the trail of development already blazed. And if there is a connection between art historical observations and ethnographic conditions,

70

we may venture the conclusion *a posteriori* that the people which cultivated Mycenean art, whether this was the Carians or a people of some other name, that this people must have formed a quite essential component of the later Greek race.'

.This opinion, in our view, misses the mark and seems in need of modification. For is the Greek element lacking from the Dipylon style?

The emergence of the Dipylon style has, with considerable justification, been linked up with the Doric migration and regarded as a partial development of that general geometric style which, according to Conze, Semper and many others, is to be considered the common property of all Aryan Indo-Germanic peoples. And as to its significance to later Greek art, Studniczka, for instance, is of an entirely different opinion. For him the geometric style of the immigrant Hellenic tribes represents the principle of strict discipline, by means of which all the borrowings from the overflowing wealth of forms from the Orient, beginning with Mycenean, were given the stamp of the genuine Hellenic spirit (*Ath. Mitteilungen*, 1887).

Here then we have opinion *versus* opinion. If we leave all other factors on one side and adhere solely to our twin criteria of abstraction and empathy, we come to the following mediatory conclusion. We recall that the principle of Mycenean art was that of enlivenment, of naturalism, whereas the Dipylon style exhibits a marked abstract tendency. Classical art now seems to us to embody a grand synthesis of these two elements, with a clear preponderance of the naturalistic element, which, during the decadent· period, became stronger and stronger and ended up as a complete travesty of the august beauty of Greek ornament. This balance between the Mycenean com-

71

ponents and the Dipylon components, this balance between naturalism and abstraction, brought to maturity that altogether felicitous result which we call Classical Greek art.

Classic Greek ornament, compared with Egyptian, shows in place of geometric regularity an organic regularity whose most sublime goal is rest in motion, living rhythm or rhythmic liveliness, in which our vital sensations can immerse themselves with complete happiness. There is no trace of naturalism in the menial sense, no trace of copying nature. We see before us pure ornament on an organic fundament. The difference between geometric regularity, i.e. regularity that owes its existence to the impulse to abstraction and organic regularity, which is voluntarily subordinate to the urge to empathy, can be most clearly defined in relation to the wavy line. I take first a purely geometrically constructed wavy line, i.e. I take a compass and join together a series of semicircles opening alternately upwards and downwards. Our empathy is unable to follow a wavy line of this nature without inhibition and contradiction. 'The movement in every semicircle, once it has begun, naturally continues along a uniform path, i.e. the semicircle is completed into a circle. By contrast, such a movement cannot, of its own accord change over into a curve in the opposite direction' (Lipps). The Greek wavy line, on the other hand, which was never extended as far as the semicircle and cannot be constructed at all with the compass, exhibits an impulse of motion which it follows in gentle undulations that correspond to our instinctive organic sensations. 'We see in it a movement that progresses in a straight line, combined with an elastic oscillation in a direction perpendicular to this. If the wavy line as a whole runs

72

horizontally, this oscillation is vertical. The upward movement always encounters in itself an elastic resistance, that is, a resistance which increases according to the law of elasticity, which brings the upward movement to a stop at a point and thereupon produces a similar downward movement, etc.' Thus the Greek wavy line is both uniform and regular, and to this extent still conforms to the abstract need; but in so far as this regularity, in contradistinction to the Egyptian regularity, is an organic one (Lipps calls it mechanical), it appeals first and foremost, with the whole of its being, to our empathy impulse.

Thus as the purest creation of the Greek artistic volition which has been characterised above, we see the living mobile festoon. 'No model in nature could have exercised an immediate influence on the coming into being of the wavy festoon, since in its two typical forms, in particular in the intermittent form, it does not occur in nature: it is a product of the Greek artistic spirit freely created out of the imagination' (Riegl). This festoon, flowing in euphonious rhythm, therefore constitutes a further development of the principle which we found above exemplified in the simple wavy line.

The difficult question of the extent to which the spiral is connected with the plant festoon shall only be touched upon here, since the conflict concerning the essence of the spiral is still ubiquitous and fierce. Analogously to the evolutionary process which we assumed for all the rest of ornamental art, we are naturally inclined to see in the spiral an originally purely geometric ornament, which slowly loses its geometric character in Greek art and ultimately approximates to the wavy festoon.

Along with the festoon the acanthus motif, which

makes its appearance during the second half of the fifth century, may be regarded as a purely Greek motif. Absurd as it is to suppose that the leaf of the *acanthus spinosus*, or bear's foot, was suddenly picked upon and made the predominant motif in the treasury of ornamental art, this assumption is nonetheless ubiquitous. It is admittedly supported by Vitruvius' anecdote concerning the genesis of the Corinthian capital, which is intimately associated with the acanthus motif. Vitruvius recounts that the chance combination of a basket and an acanthus plant which grew out of the soil beneath it, and the observation by the sculptor Callimachus of the decorative effect of this combination, were the cause of the creation of the Corinthian capital in Corinth. This shallow interpretation merely shows that in Vitruvius' time *rapport* with the authentic productive processes of a creative art instinct had been just as completely lost as it has to-day. And it is with such far-fetched and trite attempts at explanation that people hope to penetrate the *mysterium* of Greek artistic creation!

Riegl undertakes the task of proving that the acanthus did not arise along the path of direct reproduction of a natural model, but in the course of an entirely artistic process of development moving exclusively within the channels of the history of ornament. In his view the acanthus is nothing else than a palmette, or half palmette, translated into the three-dimensional medium of sculpture. Naturalisation and approximation to the plant species acanthus took place only in the course of its subsequent evolution. The reader is referred to the interesting arguments, supported by a great deal of documentary evidence, in the relevant chapter of *Stilfragen*.

We are concerned only with ascertaining the purely

ornamental value of such a motif, and so opposing the popular belief that the psychic process of artistic creation has at all times been as it appears to our own age, which is so destitute of artistic instinct, namely as a road leading from the natural model to so-called stylisation. Rather was so-called stylisation, i.e. the abstract, the linear-inanimate, the primary phenomenon, which was then refashioned in the direction of organic aliveness and so gradually came to resemble a natural model.

It would be exceeding the framework of this essay to demonstrate how the ornament of other times and other peoples fits into the viewpoints we have chosen. It has been our aim, by comparing Egyptian and Greek ornament, firstly to prove the importance and the practical utility of the questions we have posed, and secondly to lay bare, in the persons of two of the principle representatives, the two major currents that run through the whole of ornamental art. We shall now devote a few final words to the arabesque, which played such an important part in the medieval Orient, and on the other hand to the linear mode of decoration of the medieval Northern peoples. The majority of investigators construe the Saracenic arabesque as being genetically related to the Greek festoon. We are concerned only with the character of the new ornament. We find by analysis that this Saracenic ornament also represents a balance between abstraction and naturalism, but with a predominance of abstraction as pronounced as the predominance of naturalism in Greek ornament. 'If the aim of Greek art was the animation of the palmette festoons, that of the Saracenic artists seems, conversely, to have been schematisation, geometricisation, abstraction' (Riegl). The detailed process of this geometricisation may be followed in the relevant chapter of *Stilfragen*. Here we shall quote only the passage in which Riegl summarises the whole evolution as he sees it. 'The point of departure for plant ornament in the Orient (Egypt) was the geometric spiral, to which floral motifs were added as mere accessory space-fillers. Out of this the Greeks formed the living festoon, upon whose shoots and terminations they set beautifully articulated blossoms. In the Saracenic Middle Ages the Oriental spirit of abstraction, for which the trail had already been blazed afresh in the Late Antique period, once more made itself felt in the re-geometricisation of the festoon. To be sure, the fundamental achievements of the Greeks—the rhythmic undulating festoon and the free sweep across wide areas—were never again relinquished, the latter even being expanded in a certain direction. But the geometric element ubiquitously forced its way to the front again.'

The same spirit of abstraction, which was again prevalent in the early Middle Ages and was expressed in the arabesque, also gave autonomous standing to the simple interlacing strapwork ornament which, in Greek art, had been employed merely for the subordinate purposes of the border. This purely geometrical pattern, devoid of meaning and expression, was already in use during the late Roman, i.e. early Christian era, for filling in large areas, and gradually became an autonomous and self-sufficient main motif of decoration. Here then the last remnant of organic life was obliterated and purely geometric life-alien abstraction became dominant.

It is, however, different with the interlaced strapwork style of ornament that dominated the whole North of Europe during the first millenium A.D. In spite of the purely linear, inorganic basis of this ornamental style, we hesitate to term it abstract. Rather is it impossible to mistake the restless life contained in this tangle of lines. This unrest, this seeking, has no organic life that draws us gently into its movement; but there is life there, a vigorous, urgent life, that compels us joylessly to follow its movements. Thus, on an inorganic fundament, there is heightened movement, heightened expression. Here we have the decisive formula for the whole medieval North. Here are the elements which later on, as we shall show, culminate in Gothic. The need for empathy of this inharmonious people does not take the nearest-at-hand path to the organic, because the harmonious motion of the organic is not sufficiently expressive for it; it needs rather that uncanny pathos which attaches to the animation of the inorganic. The inner disharmony and unclarity of these peoples, situated far before knowledge and living in a harsh and repellent nature, could have borne no clearer fruit. We shall return to this phenomenon in our discussion of Gothic.

CHAPTER FOUR

Selected examples from
Architecture and Sculpture from the viewpoints
of Abstraction and Empathy

THIS chapter aims, without making any claim to
completeness, to sketch the major lines which
lead from the Antique to the post-Christian era,
in order, in the final chapter, to analyse under these
premises the so differentiated artistic volition of the
Middle Ages.

In the foregoing chapter we defined Greek ornament
as a thoroughly felicitous balance between abstract
and naturalistic tendencies with a strongly marked
preponderance of the latter. Since we see in the absolute artistic volition of a people the direct fruit of its
psychic disposition, we can in principle extend a definition that we have read off from the paradigm of
ornament without more ado to all the other branches
of art. Or, more accurately, we shall find our definition
of the artistic volition, arrived at by an analysis of
ornament, corroborated by the other types of art.

The disposition to abstraction which, with the Greeks
as with all other peoples, stands at the commence-
ment of the practice of art, was so rapidly pushed
into second place amongst this people of joyful tem-
perament by delight in the organic, which finally

drowned it entirely, that we may confine our investigation to demonstrating what powerful expression the abstract principle nonetheless found, particularly at the beginning of the epoch. Indeed, because the prevalence of the naturalistic organic principle is so striking, it seems to us a great deal more interesting to search out the traces of an abstract tendency, which are nevertheless present. Archaic Greek art was still clearly in the grip of abstract tendencies, and it would require an intensive investigation to analyse the processes by which, in relatively so short a time, the endowment of the Greeks with its devotion to the organic worked itself free of these abstract fetters and within a century hastened to the goal of its authentic artistic volition, a movement that proceeds almost synchronously in architecture, sculpture, and vase-painting.

An example from architecture may elucidate the situation. A comparison between the Doric and the Ionic temple will at once show the way in which the abstract principle was displaced by the organic. The Doric temple represents the product of an artistic volition still directed towards the abstract. Its inner constitution, if we may call it that, is still based on a purely geometric, or rather stereometric, inexpressive regularity, beyond whose clearly described boundaries it has no wish to go. The laws of its construction are still none other than the laws of matter. This abstract inner constitution gives it that earnest heaviness, that compactness, lifelessness, that immutable subjection to the spell of matter, which go to make up its unparalleled solemnity. Only in individual details is this abstract habitus loosened up by organic tendencies that already presage its future evolution. Amongst these, as Woermann too points out, are to be numbered the alternation of straight and sinuous lines, the curves,

79

the slight swellings in the horizontal beams, the swelling out (entasis) and tapering of the column-shafts, the slight inward inclination of the outer columns, the narrowing of the corner-transoms and the irregularity in the placing of the triglyphs. With all these trends a slight rift has already appeared in the spell of rigid abstract regularity. In the Ionic temple this shift to the organic is already fully manifest. Here matter no longer obeys its own laws only, but becomes subservient, along with its laws, to a will to art which is informed with feeling for the organic. The earnest and majestic monumentality of the Doric temple, which, with its unapproachable supra-human abstraction, weighed down the terrestrial and gave it to feel the nothingness of its humanity, is no longer to be found in the Ionic temple. Despite all its majesty and despite its gigantic masses, it stands in closer relationship to man. It rises up serene and pleasant, replete with self-confident life and striving, which, tempered by a marvellous harmony, appeals with gentle force to our sense of life. The laws of its construction are, of course, still the laws of matter, but its inner life, its expression, its harmony fall within the regularity of the organic. The compactness and rigidity of the Doric temple has been broken through; the proportions come closer to human or universally organic proportions; the columns have grown taller and more slender, they seem to rise aloft by their own force and at their topmost extremities willingly to allow themselves to be pacified by the pediment construction. Whereas in the Doric temple the lofty, expressionless law of matter in its exclusivity frightens away all human empathy, in the Ionic temple all the sensations of life flow uninhibitedly in, and the joyfulness of these stones irradiated with life becomes our own joy.

In the ensuing pages we shall have plenty of opportunity of gauging the artistic volition of a people from its architecture, and in this context we should like to enter a plea for the consideration of architectonic evolution from more elevated standpoints. That such a way of considering it is still rare may be attested by the example of Lamprecht. Notwithstanding his sensitive and modern approach to matters of art, this historian still tends to under-estimate the artistic element in architecture when he writes: 'It must be borne in mind that architecture, apart from its more or less ornamental accessories, such as the comprehension of space, which is dependent upon current cultural needs, is essentially only the embodiment of the history of a particular tectonic idea; in its core, therefore, it represents not so much the aesthetic as the logical evolution of mathematico-physical relationships. Such an evolution, however, cannot be of decisive significance for the psychological characterisation of a particular stage of development.' Lamprecht overlooks the fact that even here the tectonic idea, utilitarian purpose, and material are only factors with which a higher idea is expressed, and that within the logical evolution of a tectonic idea a corresponding gamut of psychic conditions is also being played out.

Before we now turn to sculpture, we must remind the reader of the principle which we sought to lay bare in the theoretical section. In agreement with Riegl we made the assertion that the artistic volition of the ancient cultural peoples impelled them to approximate the artistic representation to a plane, because in the plane the tactile nexus was most strictly preserved and because, for this reason, the sought after depiction of external things in their closed material individuality was most readily given expression within the plane.

The way in which this surface principle dominates art is shown pre-eminently by Egyptian art, especially Egyptian relief. But the history of Greek relief, whose significance and decisive role have been grossly underestimated, because sculpture in the round has received exclusive attention, also shows how representation in the plane was chosen not in answer to dictates from without, but for its own sake, because it was in the closest conformity with the artistic volition. Indeed, it may be said that the original and most immediately appropriate mode of expression for the Greek artistic volition was the relief. It is true that consistent pursuit of this representation in the plane was relaxed simultaneously with the naturalistic animation of archaic rigidity; shadows and foreshortening were admitted, but this tendency to relaxation never went so far as to deprive the single form of its material individuality by the introduction of free space and, in conjunction with it, of perspective. This development is reserved rather for the Post-Christian epoch. This is not what concerns us here however. Rather let us seek, under these premises, to do justice to Antique, and especially archaic and archaicising Greek sculpture from a fresh point of view. We shall here advocate the standpoint, which may appear paradoxical, but which follows clearly from the presuppositions, that round-sculptural representation is a type of art which is due to external conditions and runs counter to the original abstract artistic volition, whereas the kind of art that arises out of the original abstract artistic volition is precisely representation in the plane.

And here it is only monumental sculpture that comes under consideration. Miniature sculpture naturally serves better for the satisfaction of an imitative play impulse that rejoices in symbols and upon whose productions other demands are made than upon a work of art. Nevertheless, the stylistic elements of monumental sculpture can also be demonstrated in miniature sculpture, even though they do not find there an equally forceful expression.

In the great monumental art then, the demand for round-sculptural representation appears as an inhibitive factor for the authentic artistic volition. That is to say: where external circumstances and conditions demanded round-sculptural representation, the problem was one of overcoming the resistances arising out of this demand; in other words, of carrying out the principles of the artistic volition, despite this resistance. We shall discuss in a moment the way in which this will was able to force its way through. It may however be noted in anticipation that it is in this original incompatibility of round-sculptural representation with the dictates of an artistic volition directed toward the abstract, toward eternalisation, that the reason must be sought for the phenomenon that all sculpture in the round bears most strongly the marks of a so-called stylisation. Because, with its three-dimensionality, which at once draws it into relativity and the unclarity of appearances, it threatens to escape from that urge to eternalisation which is contained at varying degrees of strength in every artistic volition, it has to be eternalised with all the more vigorous external means. It is relatively simple to wrest the things of the outer world from the flux of happening and to render them perceptible *per se* in their material individuality and closed unity by projecting them onto a plane surface; but the means of sculpture in the round are ill-adapted to this aim, for in truth a free-sculptural representation occupies just as lost and arbitrary a position in the world-picture as its natural model, which the artist has simply tried to eternalise in stone. Naturally he seeks to achieve this eternalisation along another route than by simply translating the model into an indestructible material. Where he contents himself with this latter procedure he ends up with a lump of stone, but no work of art.

The means that were found of bridging or suppressing the inevitable contradiction between round-sculptural representation and abstract tendencies to eternalisation, constitute the history of the evolution of the idea of sculptural style. Two main factors in this process can be most easily picked out. There arose the postulate to give a different form of expression to the notion of material individuality, which had otherwise been attained only through the tactile nexus of the plane surface. This came about through the attempt to preserve this impression of unity and the tactile nexus as far as possible by the compactness of the material and its undivided corporeality. This fundamental law of sculpture has remained unchanged from the earliest archaic statues to Michelangelo, Rodin and Hildebrand. For there is, in principle, no difference between an archaic statue and one of Michelangelo's tomb-figures. In the former the figure seems to grow laboriously out of a column, the arms adhere closely to the body, as far as possible all division of the surface is avoided and divisions that are unavoidable are either intimated in a general way only or else merely painted on, in order to achieve the maximum impression of material compactness. In contradistinction to this, with Michelangelo the compactness of matter is rendered perceptible not from without, but from within. In his case the strictly terminal limits of matter are not factual but imaginary, yet we are nonetheless clearly conscious of them. We cannot touch them, but we feel them with their cubic compactness. For it is only under the invisible pressure of this cubic compactness that the dynamism of Michelangelo's formal language acquires its superhuman grandeur. Within a closed cubic space a maximum of movement; here we have one of the formulas of Michelangelo's art. This formula comes alive for us when we recall the incubus, the oppressive dream, that lies over all these figures, the tormented, impotent desire to tear oneself free, which lifts every creation of Michelangelo's spirit into a realm of profound and gigantic tragedy. Thus whereas the compactness of matter is physically tangible in the archaic figure, with Michelangelo we feel only the invisible cubic form in which his figures pursue their existence. The goal is the same in both, however, namely to approximate the representation to material individuality and closed unity.

The artistic materialists naturally failed to see these deeper causes of the genesis of sculptural style; they explained all constraint by the resistance of the material. They were never struck by the absurdity of the idea that the chisel which exactly hacked out the face of an archaic figure, or the minute decorations of its vestments, should not have possessed the ability to separate the arms or the legs from the body and give these limbs some sort of support. Why put such a simple explanation, which is so illuminating to sound commonsense, to the test? To be sure, a fleeting glance at Egyptian sculptures would already have revealed the untenability of such a thesis. That the Egyptians had acquired an easy mastery over material is shown by the statues of the secular art of the Old Empire, which have been sufficiently admired for their realism —the village mayor, the brewer etc. And at the same time the statues in the court style, that is the authentic monumental art, exhibits an undividedness of form and a severity of style as great as any archaic statue. Something else must, therefore, have contributed to this style than technical incompetence, as the artistic materialists would have us believe. Riegl says: 'We have no wish to deny the fact that a progressive development has taken place since Egyptian art, but a protest must be raised against the belief that this development was one of technical ability. In pure technical ability, i.e. in the mastery of raw materials, the Egyptians were superior to their successors right up to the present day' (*Spätrömische Kunstindustrie*).

After this digression we will repeat the first postulate of sculptural artistic volition: tactile compactness of material. We shall acquaint ourselves with the second postulate at once. It is entirely in concord with the course of development which we formulated theoretically in Part One when Collignon says in his history of Greek sculpture: 'The first symbols of the Godhead, the so-called aniconic images, irrespective of whether they were carved out of wood or stone, were purely geometrical in form; they can be reduced to a few very simple types. Such were the basic elements from which, in the course of development, the first Greek statues proceeded. They still make their presence felt in the archaic statue and in the homely votive offering modelled out of clay.' According to this then, the first symbols of the Godhead were pure abstractions, without any resemblance to life. It was clear that as soon as a real natural model was found worthy of being rendered in monumental sculpture, the attempt was made to approximate this rendering to the former pure abstraction. Let the reader recall how, in Part One, we sought to define the work of art of early epochs, in so far as a natural model underlay it, as a compromise

86

between the urge to abstraction and the very necessity of reproducing the natural model. And let him compare with this definition Schmarsow's statements in his chapter on monumental sculpture: 'Every inflection of the strictly geometric figure, every approximation to the forms of the plant or animal world softens and weakens the ruthless clarity of the monumental tectonic and carries the figures involved over into the conditions of growth and life, i.e. of temporality. The representation of organic creatures seems to stand in incompatible contradiction to this abstract eternalisation of existence in the crystalline body. The figure of an organic growth already proclaims manifold relationship, betrays in every member the conditionality of growing and withering. The mobility of organisms opposes all interpretation as fixed form. How far removed is the living individual from the absolute closedness of the regular body, and yet the project is undertaken of separating the values of existence from those of life and eternalising that element in the organic growth which can be rendered as a permanent component in rigid material. Forcible accommodation to the framework of cubic forms is the first maxim of this monumental endeavour, once the artist has become conscious that it is a matter not of imitating reality, not of representing the living creature in its actions and activities, in its relation to nature, but, on the contrary, of abstracting the constant, of transcribing the living into the immobile, rigid, cold and impenetrable—of recreating it in another, an inorganic nature' (*Grundbegriffe der Kunstwissenschaft*, Chapter XVI). Here too then the compromise character of the sculptural work of art is clearly underlined.

To call for aid upon the laws of the inorganic in order to raise the organic into a timeless sphere, to eternalise it, is a law of all art, but exceptionally so of sculpture. This embellishment of the organic with the inorganic may take place in a variety of ways. The one that lies closest to hand is forcibly to press the forms into tectonic values, to enclose them as it were in a tectonic regularity, within which their authentic life is suppressed. Heinrich Brunn, in his *Kleine Schriften*, undertook a highly remarkable initial attempt to make tectonic style in Greek sculpture and painting the object of a detailed investigation. He characterises the evolution of Greek monumental sculpture as a conquest of the schematico-mechanical (i.e. the abstract-regular) by the organico-rhythmic 'and if, in the process, the tectonic principle does not lose the regulating influence which it previously exercised as an educating medium, it nevertheless withdraws, outwardly, further and further into the background, and continues to operate only more or less unconsciously and in secret' (*Kleine Schriften*, Munich, 1905). Thus the Greeks soon abandoned this forcible accommodation to the framework of cubic forms, and sought to overcome the abstract-regular by the organic-regular, dead geometric form by the rhythm of the organic. Their happy natural endowment, the joyousness that characterised their feeling for life, pointed out this route to them. The sculpture of other peoples recoiled from such enlivenment and an Egyptian would certainly have been incapable of appraising the organic beauty and harmony of a Classical statue, and would perhaps have turned away in arrogant disdain from such trifling.

In forcible accommodation to regular cubic forms, in the tectonic constraint of the figures, organic values were outwardly transposed into the world of the inorganic. This takes place in a more subtle and inward manner through the incorporation of sculpture into architecture. Here tectonic constraint is not direct, but indirect. The same principle has come to be employed in a diverse fashion. Sculpture is totally absorbed in another organism of the highest regularity. Now if this architectonic regularity is of an organic kind, as in Greek architecture, the constraint within which sculpture lives also has an organic effect, as for instance in the figures of a pediment; if, on the contrary, it is of an inorganic kind, as in Gothic, the figures are drawn into the same inorganic sphere. In the latter as in the former case, however, they lose the arbitrariness and lack of clarity which adheres to round-sculptural representation, in that, as though conscious of their relativity, they fasten onto a system of regular structure extraneous to themselves. Maximum compactness of material, forcible compression of the object into geometrical or cubic regularity: these two laws of sculptural style are to be found at the inception of all sculptural art and remain more or less determinant throughout the whole course of its evolution; because sculpture, as already stated, is, through its three-dimensionality, least able to dispense with so-called stylisation and therefore, of all the arts, bears the most distinct marks of the need for abstraction.

A third postulate, which is closely bound up with the first and is in reality merely a consistent development of it, was fulfilled only by those peoples whose artistic volition was entirely subject to the principle of abstraction. This postulate was to cause the cubic construction to give the effect of a plane surface, i.e. to work over the sculptural construct in such a way that the visual image created in the spectator the illusion of a surface representation, instead of three-dimensional reality. This tendency found expression in an outward, direct manner with the Egyptians, in an internalised, indirect one for example with Hildebrand.

We will call to mind the principles propounded in Hildebrand's *Problem der Form*. There he states: 'As long as a sculptural figure makes itself felt primarily as cubic it is still in the initial stage of configuration; only when it creates an impression of flatness, although it is cubic, does it acquire artistic form. Only through the consistent implementation of this relief interpretation of our cubic impressions does the representation gain its sacred fire, and the mysterious benison that we receive from the work of art rests upon it alone.'

The principle here enunciated by the modern sculptor was most ruthlessly implemented, as we have already stated, by the Egyptians. The perfect example of the Egyptian artistic volition is represented by the pyramid, which may equally well be regarded as a sculptural memorial or an architectonic shape. Here the aforesaid tendencies are made most severely and unequivocally manifest, and it is therefore understandable that no other people has imitated this form. Now what are the preconditions for the genesis of this peculiar form? A cubic shape was required by the practical purpose, namely the tomb-chambers. On the other hand, the construction was supposed to be a memorial, a memorial effective from a distance and solemnly impressive, that was to stand alone on a broad plane. A form had, therefore, to be found that was calculated to evoke most expressly the impression of material individuality and closed unity. To this, however, was opposed, for reasons set out earlier, the cubic framework required by the practical purpose. It was a problem therefore 'of divesting the cubic of its agonising quality', of transposing the cubic into surface impressions. The pyramid stands before us as the most consistent imaginable fulfilment of this endeavour. Let Riegl speak: 'The architectural ideal of the Ancient Egyptian undoubtedly attained its purest expression in the sepulchral memorial type of the pyramid. Before whichever of the four sides the spectator stands, his eye always perceives merely the uniform plane of the equilateral triangle, whose sharply terminal sides give no reminder of the extension in depth behind them. In comparison with this carefully considered and very acutely emphasised limitation of the outward material appearance within the surface dimensions, the actual utilitarian task—space-construction—withdraws completely into the background. It is confined to the provision of a small sepulchral vault with insignificant entrances that are as good as non-existent when looked at from without. Material individuality in the strictest Oriental sense could hardly find a more consummate expression.' Our reasons for terming the pyramid the perfect example of all abstract tendencies are evident. It gives the purest expression to them. In so far as the cubic can be transmuted into abstraction, it has been done here. Lucid rendering of material individuality, severely geometric regularity, transposition of the cubic into surface impressions: all the dictates of an extreme urge to abstraction are here fulfilled. In the *mastabas*, the tombs of the great, and on the other hand in the temple and dwelling construction of the Egyptians—to say nothing of sculpture—an analogous aspiration is everywhere in evidence. Only here the utilitarian purpose demanded greater concessions, and since it was not a question of ideal building constructions, as in the royal pyramids, concessions were all the more readily made.

How strongly Egyptian sculpture in the round, in so far as it adhered to the hieratic court style, was marked by the striving to free the spectator from the agonising relativity of the cubic, becomes clear to anyone at the most cursory glance. Wherever it was possible at all, the attempt was made to conceal dimensions of depth by plane surface constructions, to banish them from memory. This aspiration naturally met with least success in relation to the heads of the statues, especially since here a certain verisimilitude had to be achieved. For according to the belief of the Egyptains the continued life of the 'Ka' was to some extent dependent upon the verisimilitude of the image. Everywhere else, however, plane surface effects were sought after. The forefronts of the figures often appear pressed completely flat. In the sitting, or rather squatting figures the legs frequently form a cohesive, cube-shaped mass with the whole body, out of which only the shoulders project, together with the head as a necessary individual characterisation. The undivided planes of this cube are frequently covered with hieroglyphics recounting the deeds of the subject of the representation; they have thus completely lost their actual significance and have become writing surfaces. But even in details the endeavour to give the spectator the greatest possible number of plane surface impressions can be observed, for instance in the head ornament, the royal crowns, the aprons and robes etc. Finally the impression of depth is then often destroyed by setting a pillar up against the rear of the figure.

As the last and most external means of transferring the organic into the sphere of the inorganic-abstract, we may mention the tendency to treat details in a purely decorative manner, to make geometrical patterns out of them. Thus, for example, the folds of the robes are stylised into stiffness and regularity, the fall of the drapery at the hem of the robe is transformed into a surface pattern, the same with the edge of that piece of the robe which is lifted up and anywhere else that opportunity offers, as for instance in the treatment of the hair. For it is hardly to be supposed that the frequently very voluminous hair-styles were so stiffly stylised in reality; it is much more likely that plentiful use was made here of the opportunity of embellishing cubic values with abstract values—which is, of course, not intended as denial of the fact that the ancient Orientals wore elaborate hair-styles, or rather wigs.

The exceptional type of stylisation we have just mentioned plays a great part in Byzantine art, to which we shall now turn before passing on to medieval Northern art. For a consideration of the elements out of which Northern medieval art is composed demands, above all, an investigation of the art that most clearly represents the artistic volition of the first millenium A.D. And this is undoubtedly Byzantine art. The question of the historical genesis and genetic evolution of this style is one of the most difficult and interesting in the whole history of art. There is a particularly strong division of opinion as to the relative share in its development of the Indo-Germans and the Orientals. Byzantine represents first and foremost the universal legatee of Antique and Early Christian art. The fact that Riegl interprets Early Christian or Late Roman art not as a separate phenomenon motivated by the intervention of the barbarians, but as a logical developmental phase of Antique art and as a necessary transition to the art of the modern period, introduces a fresh complication. Here we must cite a somewhat lengthy passage from Riegl, because it contains many viewpoints which are also of considerable importance to the aim of our disquisition. Riegl makes the reliefs on

93

the Arch of Constantine the basis of his analysis of the Late Roman artistic volition and comes to the following conclusion: 'The Constantinian reliefs have always been found wanting in the specific and peculiar quality of the Classical reliefs, namely beautiful vitality. The figures have been deemed on the one hand ugly, and on the other heavy and immobile. This has seemed to justify the declaration that they were the work if not of barbarian hands, then of craftsmen who had fallen under barbarian influence. As regards beauty, we certainly miss that of proportion (in our terminology, of the organic), which balances each part according to size and movement with the adjacent part and with the whole; in place of this, however, we find a different sort of beauty, which achieves expression in the strictest geometrical composition and to which we may give the name of crystalline, because it constitutes the first and most eternal formal law of lifeless matter and of absolute beauty (material individuality), which can, of course, only be thought and to which the actual achievement only comes relatively close. Barbarians would undoubtedly have reproduced in misconstrued and coarsened forms of expression the law of proportional beauty inherited from Classical art; the authors of the Constantinian reliefs replaced it by a different one, and thereby gave evidence of an autonomous artistic volition. To be sure, this lofty regular beauty is not a living beauty. On the other hand, the figures of these reliefs are by no means lacking in liveliness— only this does not lie in the tactile modelling of the limb junctures (joints), and not at all in the tactile and normal-visual modelling of the nude or of drapery, but in the lively alternation of light and dark, the effect of which is especially vivid from a distance. Thus vitality is present and indeed extreme, because it rests on a

94

momentary optical impression, but it is not a beautiful vitality (according to Classical concepts, i.e. based on tactile modelling in half-shadows). From these brief and general indications we can already reach the conclusion that in the Constantinian reliefs the two targets of all plastic artistic creation—beauty and verisimilitude—were just as much striven after and also, in fact, achieved, as in Classical art; but whereas in the latter they were fused into a harmonious equipoise (beautiful vitality), they have now split up into their extremes again: on the one hand the loftiest regular beauty in the strictest form of crystallinism, on the other verisimilitude in the most extreme form of the momentary optical effect' (*Spätrömische Kunstindustrie*, page 48f.). These arguments, with whose conclusions we cannot immediately agree, provide us with two facts that are of importance to our method of investigation. Above all we find confirmation of the fact that the unity of the work of art is here again sought in its crystalline-geometric regularity, and therefore that its inner constitution is again abstract. It is true that this fact is obscured through the continued utilisation by this changed artistic volition of detailed Antique achievements, that, so to speak, it continues to play on the same instrument; on the other hand, this very circumstance forces all the more energetically into consciousness its difference from pure Antique.

A further important fact is furnished by the colouristic effect as defined above by Riegl. There can be no doubt that here shadow, which in the Antique relief was only a means to an end without a function of its own, has itself become an artistic medium. It serves as a compositional factor, and thus supplements the crystalline regularity. To designate this carefully thought out alternation of light and dark a means to the attainment of verisimilitude, as Riegl does—correct as it is from Riegl's point of view—might lead to misconceptions. It is true that the plane surface is unquestionably given life by this interaction, but this liveliness proceeds according to abstract principles, so that the overall impression becomes increasingly that of a pattern. And this kind of colourism makes no appeal to our capacity for empathy. This is the crucial factor. As a compositional means in an organic sense the alternation of light and shade becomes akin only in later epochs of artistic development where, transferred to painting, it ends in the pictorial problems of our own time, after passing along the magnificent line that leads from Piero della Francesca and Leonardo *via* Rubens to Rembrandt and Velasquez.

Thus in the two factors we encounter in Early Christian art, the specific common *novum* is clearly revealed as the tendency to the abstract. It can hardly be contested that this *novum* is associated with the new spirit which entered the Roman world through Christianity. In its spirit Christianity is of Oriental-Semitic provenance; it was therefore bound also to bring to expression in its artistic volition the abstract trends prevalent in the Semitic East.

Alongside the whole Hellenic development Byzantine art now also absorbed the elements of Early Christian art, and worked them up into a composite art in which Hellenistic, Early Christian and universal Oriental were united to the accompaniment of much internal conflict, into a new style which, bearing this complexion, attained a sort of world dominion. It is not altogether correct to speak of the total suppression of any of these components, as is intimated by Strzygowski's slogan 'Hellas in the embrace of the Orient'; rather do the last threads of Antique artistic evolution terminate here as unhindered and logically as Early Christian and Oriental art forge their way to this stage of development. The Early Christian stylistic elements had naturally not remained confined to Roman and Western soil, but, along with Christianity itself, had spread to Egypt (Coptic art) and Hither Asia; here they were fused with the indigenous art of kindred tendency and passed over thus into Byzantine art.

The vacillation between Hellenic-organic tradition and this Early Christian-Oriental abstract influence constituted the history of the evolution of Byzantine art, until the dispute ended with victory for the un-Antique abstract elements through the mighty advance of Islam.

During this period the evolution of artistic volition proceeded in fits and starts between contradictory extremes, as though in a series of convulsions; this is sufficiently explained by the violence and wealth of conflict with which here, in the Eastern Roman world empire, races and peoples met and mingled with one another. The cardinal phases of this evolution are well known. During the Theodosian age abstract tendencies, as expressed in the geometricisation of decoration, particularly of Antique plant motifs, and in the diminution of the feeling for form, enjoyed a pronounced supremacy. Instead of sculptural modelling, we find flat engraving with a pattern-like alternation of light and dark. This development continued during the period of Justinian. Then came the centuries of the iconoclasm, which seem to have brought in their train a standstill in all fields. 'Of the two centuries between Justinian and Charlemagne, this much can be said with certainty: they one-sidedly sought the value of a work of art in its immaterial subject matter to a greater extent than has been the case at any other time. During the era of the rise of Islam, while iconoclasm was raging, the Christian view of culture also drew considerably closer to the Jewish, which had declared creation that competed with nature to be untrustworthy and inimical to harmony, i.e. that plastic art, in so far as it related to the imitation of animate creatures, was *per se* inartistic' (Riegl, *Spätrömische Kunstindustrie*). Then we are suddenly surprised by a vigorous resurgence of Antique-Hellenistic tendencies. The organic again dominates artistic volition. To this period belong, for example, the narthex mosaics of the Church of St. Sophia in Constantinople and, in the province of illuminated manuscripts, the celebrated Codex 139 of the National Library in Paris with its sumptuous illuminations. But with the two centuries long dominion of the Macedonian Empire this reburgeoning of organic sensibility also came to an end. If this epoch of Byzantine art represents the florescence of its Indo-German-Antique constituent, the constituent originating from the opposite, the Oriental-abstract pole had its florescence during the first centuries of the second millenium, when Byzantium was under the sway of the Comnenian emperors. It is undoubtedly in this form that Byzantine art has exercised the strongest influence on the West, which has led to the erroneous equation of this late Comnenian art with Byzantium art as a whole.

Artistic estimation of this Comnenian art is of very recent date. Previously its conscious artistic volition was almost completely overlooked and nothing was seen in it but lack of artistic power, the epithets 'schematic', 'lifeless', 'rigid' were not only statements of fact, but also the expression of an unfavourable value-judgement. This was because everyone was completely under the spell of a view of art which had derived its aesthetic from the Antique and the Renaissance, and had consequently made the organic-true-to-life the criterion of its evaluations. The supposition that the goal of art might be sought in the lifeless, in the rigid, was out of the question from the standpoint of the earlier science of art. The detailed and brilliant analysis of Byzantine art given by Semper in his *Stil* was, or course, based entirely on his materialist theory; it linked up the peculiar quality of Byzantine art with carpet-weaving, without pausing to consider the possibility that a particular technique was selected because it was in the closest accord with the artistic volition. The first decisive advance in the objective appraisal of Byzantine style was made by Robert Vischer with his essay *Kritik der mittelalterlichen Kunst*, published in his collected *Studien*. Here, despite all his 'Europo-centric' bias (if, just for once, we may be permitted this neologism analogous to geo-centric) and materialist views, he does at least attempt to demonstrate a positive artistic aspiration in the Byzantine style. We will quote a few passages from this treatise which, at the same time, furnish a characterisation of the style itself: 'The transformation of Late Byzantine pictorial art into the planimetric and stereometric decorative is without any doubt to be explained by a deterioration of art, by a numbing of the feeling for organic corporeality (which is thus here clearly identified with art as a whole), just as much as by a sharpening of the feeling for surface decoration and architectonic. Hence we have to do, from the point of view of a critique of value also, with a peculiar commingling, with a blend of art and the inartistic, of artistic purpose and tricks of craftsmanship. The schematic element is in one respect the inevitable outcome of helpless clumsiness and ignorance [*sic!*], and in another respect is freely desired and executed with style.'

One feels how, in this analysis, a new outlook is struggling with the old, and how every concession made to the new is rescinded again by the old.

A further passage runs:

'This style consists in a decorative externalisation and schematisation of the figure, an approximation of the human image to the character of surface ornament and thereby to architectonic constraint. That the human figure with its formal value should also be subjected to such an abstraction is certainly strange, but not preposterous. For the de-organisation of the organic enters into the work to the advantage of a style which is essentially decorative in nature; thus it has its meaning, and within this meaning also an aesthetic effect. All pictorial art has a subjectivist propensity, which leads it to a relatively independent attitude toward the given natural model and seeks expression in purely formal terms, in forms as such; hence all pictorial art has a profound relationship to decoration and a greater or lesser inclination to the playful refashioning of natural structures, as it were toward drowning the sound of singing with orchestral music. Thus the artist came gradually and quite simply to impose upon the living figure the character of surface ornament. The total appearance of the human figure, giving expression to its autonomous, closed organic life, was now replaced by an harmonious conglomerate of particles, in which the aim of giving an illusion of life takes second place to the aim of achieving an autonomous decorative effect.'

So far does Vischer's understanding of the Byzantine style go. He does not reach complete understanding because he gives to the word 'decorative' only the superficial interpretation we are accustomed to, and thus overlooks the deeper content of this artistic volition, which would be more fittingly designated 'ornamental'.

This is not the place for a detailed analysis of Byzantine art. We are here concerned only with our particular viewpoints and with the significance of the style for the further development of Northern European art. And there it can already be clearly seen from Vischer's characterisation that in this art the whole tendency was once more abstract; it sought as far as possible to evade the organic as a clouding of eternity-value and once more avoided three-dimensionality with fully conscious intention, seeking all salvation in the plane surface.

This is the point at which to deduce the psychic presuppositions of such an artistic volition from the religion and world view of the people in question, and so to lay bare by an example the intimate relationship between art and religion, as two coequal expressions of the same psychic disposition, of the same *température d'âme*.

To the polar contrast between empathy and abstraction, which we found applicable to the consideration of art, correspond in the domain of the history of religion and of world views the two concepts of intra-mundaneity (immanence), which is characterised as polytheism or pantheism, and supra-mundaneity (transcendence), which leads over to monotheism.

Confident surrender to the outer world, the sensuously secure feeling of being at ease and at one with creation, the whole of this temperate and felicitous mental climate of the Greeks, expressed in their world-revering pantheism, was bound—if psychic motives for the genesis of a work of art are accepted at all— to lead to that Classical style whose beauty is living and organic, into which the need for empathy, un-restrained by any anxieties concerning the world, could flow without let or hindrance. It is true of both religious and aesthetic experience: it was objectified self-enjoyment. Man was at home in the world and felt himself its centre. Man and world were not anti-theses and, sustained by this faith in the reality of appearances, a comprehensive sensory-intellectual mas-tery of the world-picture was arrived at. All Greek philosophy, in so far as it is free of Asiatic-Oriental admixtures, is an extension of the surface of the visible world from the central point of the contemplating and thinking man; that is why its systems have furnished modern humanity with such vast material for a ration-alistic interpretation of the universe. It may well be said that it was the Greeks who first taught mankind to think scientifically, and that the whole of our modern thought and concept-formation is still under the spell of this Greek philosophy and its sequel, scholasticism, or to name the representatives of these systems, under the spell of an Aristotelian-Thomasinian world view.

The criterion of a disturbed relationship between man and outer world is the transcendent complexion of religious notions with its consequence, the dualistic severance of spirit and matter, of this world and the next. Naïve sensuous oneness with nature is replaced by a disunion, a relationship of fear between man and world, a scepticism toward the surface and appearance of things, above and beyond which the ultimate cause of things, an ultimate truth was sought. This world with its reality could not suffice the profound instinct for the impenetrability of creation and for the prob-lematic nature of all appearance. And out of this instinct the peoples with a transcendental cast of spirit created a world beyond. All transcendental religions are, by nature, more or less markedly religions of redemption; they seek to bring redemption from the conditionality of human being and from the conditionality of the phenomenal world. Are many more words needed to prove that this *température d'âme* renders all artistic activity abstract? Was this urge to abstraction anything else than the striving to create resting-points within the flight of appearances, necessities within the arbitrary, redemption from the anguish of the relative? It is evident that transcendental notions in a religious respect, and the urge to abstraction in an artistic respect, are expressions of the same psychic disposition *vis-à-vis* the cosmos. And this psychic disposition, which impeded the development of art in the direction of the organic-naturalistic, also preserved the Oriental spirit from a development of its world view in the direction of Greek rationalism. And now we are in a position to place a different valuation upon the fact that Greek art made no headway in the East, especially not in Egypt—just as little as Greek thought succeeded in changing the fundamental nature of Eastern wisdom. Rather was it absorbed by the latter. Greece and Egypt, notwithstanding their numerous cultural contacts, must be regarded as the most rigorous representatives of opposite world views. And in consequence of this their artistic volitions also evince a polar antithesis.

Religious transcendence and its configuration most familiar to us, Christianity, are of Oriental provenance. The Greek pantheon had long since been infiltrated by transcendental Oriental notions, before Christianity assisted these elements, in a new setting, to victory on the soil of Rome. The reaction of this transcendental sensibility upon artistic volition is clearly manifest in the abstract tendency of Early Christian art as described above in terms of the Constantinian reliefs.

Ancient Roman culture then on the one hand consciously fostered its Hellenic inheritance, while on the other it made Christianity the State religion. During the Comnenian period, however, Antique recollections were completely silenced, and under the influence of nascent Islam, that late after-growth of the religion-forming power of the Semitic race as Pfleiderer[15] calls it, the transcendental tendencies gained sole sovereignty, which led to Late Byzantine art, unmistakable in its purely abstract habitus.

In the elements comprising this art: return to the plane surface, suppression of the organic, crystalline-geometric composition, we find the basic components of Ancient Oriental Egyptian art once more. The circle seems to be closed again and Graeco-Roman art has almost the appearance of a comparatively brief interruption of a permanent condition, of a firmly established type of art. And yet how different does Byzantine art prove to be from Ancient Egyptian, how clearly it reveals the fact that it has passed through the Antique phase of development. This is not the place to examine the principal factors in this diversity of essence —the new achievements of Early Christian and Byzantine art as disclosed by Riegl and Strzygowski and relating primarily to the problem of space, the shift from tactile objectivism to optical objectivism (Riegl), and colourism. An external consideration may serve to instruct us concerning this diversity. Compare a Byzantine relief of the good period with an Ancient Egyptian relief, and finally with a Greek vase decoration. Despite the fact that the purely geometric-abstract setting and the markedly abstract tendency bring the Byzantine work quite close to the Egyptian, we nevertheless notice at once, by the elegance and beauty of the linear-ornamental construction, by the gracefulness of arrangement, often amounting to delicacy, that the course of development has passed through Greek art, as we see it, for example, in any random vase decoration.

CHAPTER FIVE

Northern Pre-Renaissance Art

IN Late Byzantine art, the influence of which is un-
disputed though opinions differ as to its extent, we
have only *one* premise for the style-genetic development of Western Pre-Renaissance art. Having, in the
previous chapter, characterised this Byzantine artistic
volition as far as is important to our purpose, we must
turn to the other premises. Here the first question
to arise is how that indigenous artistic activity, which
is present independently of Antique and Oriental-
Byzantine influence, is to be regarded in the light of
our viewpoints. It is true that we can hardly speak of
a fully-evolved Northern art; but nonetheless we can
deduce from the existing first steps toward an artistic
activity, from the configurations of the initial inner
formative impulse, a quite distinct and peculiar artistic
volition. By this we mean Northern Celto-Germanic
decorative art, as manifested in the ornament of the
Scandinavian and Irish North, in the style of the
Migration of the Peoples and in Merovingian art,
which despite local variations constitutes a quite distinct artistic direction. All the artistic volition of these
peoples finds its gratification within this ornamental
art, and so we may, with Sophus Müller, identify the
art of the Northern peoples with their ornament.

Now what is characteristic of this ornament, as we indicated in Chapter Three, is the absolute predominance of linear-geometric form, which excludes every hint of the organic. The connection with the primal beginnings of Greek and Oriental art is therefore given. The diversity is all the easier to analyse. This latter is rooted in the universal *état d'âme*.

Northern man's relationship to nature was undoubtedly not that state of familiarity which we found amongst the Greeks; on the other hand, however, his feeling for the world does not exhibit the same profundity as that of the ancient Oriental cultural peoples. The naïve Northern nature religion, with its cloudy mysticism, knew nothing of that deep dread which we felt in the Oriental-Semitic religion of transcendence. It stood *before* cognition, whereas the religion of the Oriental stood *above* cognition. The Northern peoples experienced within a harsh and unyielding nature the resistance of this nature, their isolation within it, and they confronted the things of the outer world and their appearance full of disquiet and distrust. No clear blue sky arched above them, no serene climate, no luxuriant vegetation surrounded them, to induce in them a world-revering pantheism. A repellent nature precluded the emergence of that secure sensuous instinct which is necessary before man can surrender himself to nature with confidence. The consequence was an inner disharmony, and it was this which steeped all religious notions in dualistic elements and hence rendered the North so incapable of resistance to the penetration of Christianity.

For Northern mysticism had so little inner stability, so closely resembled the mist before sunrise, that it shrank back helpless before Roman practical rationalism, that carried in its wake Christianity as the State religion; filled with a befitting respect for the alien reason and the alien religion, it crept into all sorts of nooks and crannies. In contrast to Oriental mysticism, which was more than mere mist before sunrise, which was the most profound consciousness of the unfathomableness of the world. Northern man felt only a veil betwixt nature and himself, a veil that he believed he would one day be able to raise. The problematic nature of all cognition had not yet dawned on him.

From this *état d'âme* it followed that the artistic volition of Northern man, on the one hand, was perforce abstract, but that on the other it could not have the intensity and high urgency of the Oriental. No doubt there was sufficient disquiet *vis-à-vis* the outer world, sufficient inner isolation from nature to check any familiarity and thereby all feeling for the organic. And therefore artistic volition was exclusively dominated by the inorganic, as shown by the so-called strapwork and animal ornament.

Yet all these linear-geometric convolutions are never reduced to the simplest abstract formula, never carried through to clear necessity and regularity; rather is there expression in them, a seeking and striving that goes beyond abstract tranquillity and exclusivity. This complicated, opaque, and seemingly arbitrary mode of linear decoration could never have satisfied the artistic volition of Oriental peoples. Here there was, so to speak, merely the material for abstraction, but never abstraction itself. All the restless searching and striving after knowledge, all the inner disharmony appears in this heightened expression of the inanimate. The lucid consciousness of the impossibility of knowledge, absolute passive resignation, had led the Oriental artistic volition to that expressionless tranquillity and necessity of the abstract; here in the North, however, there is anything but tranquillity, here an inner need for expression desires, in spite of all the inner disharmony —or rather all the more so because of it—to speak itself out. We will recall what was said in Chapter Three: 'It is impossible to mistake the restless life contained in this tangle of lines. This unrest, this seeking, has no organic life that draws us gently into its movement; but there is life there, a tormenting, urgent life that compels us joylessly to follow its movements. Thus on an inorganic fundament there is heightened movement, heightened expression. This is the decisive formula for the whole medieval North. The inner need for life and empathy of these inharmonious peoples did not take the nearest-at-hand path to the organic, because the peaceful, balanced movement of the organic had no sufficient message for them, because their disharmony could not express itself through the medium of the organic; it needed rather the intensification of a resistance, it needed that uncanny pathos which attaches to the animation of the inorganic.' And so that contradictory, hybrid formation comes into being: abstraction on the one hand, and most vigorous expression on the other.

It is the same heightened pathos that finds expression in all mechanical imitation of organic functions, as for example in marionettes.

The diversity of Northern linear constructions from the linear artistic efforts of the Egyptians, who were fully satisfied with linear design that lacked all expression, is obvious.

The way in which, in Northern ornament, animal motifs become geometrical patterns, in which everything organic is drawn into the expression of their lines, is well known. The same fate naturally also befell the representation of human figures, as it occurs at an advanced stage in the development of this art, e.g. in illuminated manuscripts. The difference from Egyptian linear drawing is clearly manifest. Let us read how Woermann describes this Northern artistic activity: 'The animal motifs are wedded to the motifs of interlacing ribbons. The quadrupeds appear to be pulled apart into ribbons, the heads of the birds are set on long, ribbon-like necks. Above all, however, the human figures, pulled apart and dispersed, participate in the general calligraphic ferment. Even where the figures of the saints occupy the centre as the principal images, they are kept flat and schematic. The hair of their beards and heads is dissolved into ribbons with rolled up ends. Their limbs are stunted. As in primitive art they are seen either entirely full-face or entirely in profile. Their vestments become rolls of ribbon, their features geometrical lines' (Woermann, *Geschichte der Kunst, II Band*, 87).

This proclivity to the inorganic line, to the life-negating form, naturally met half way the abstract tendency exhibited, on the one hand, by the Early Christian art disseminated by the monasteries and, on the other, by Late Byzantine art. Out of the confusion of an evolution that went on for centuries and was exposed to the most varied currents, the first relatively clear and distinct result to appear is the Romanesque style. The major factors in its composition are the following: firstly, the direct patrimony of Roman provincial art, secondly the Early Christian canon propagated by the monasteries, thirdly Byzantine art, and fourthly the indigenous artistic volition of the Northern peoples analysed above. From the composition alone it can be inferred that little scope was left for the organic within this style, especially as the organic-Antique inheritance was taken over as an uncomprehended form and partially debased by barbarian influence. Nevertheless, sensible of the superiority of Roman art, artists adhered outwardly very closely to this inherited type. Indeed, as is well known, the Carolingian period even saw a conscious renascence of the Antique.

The Romanesque and Gothic styles cannot be looked at in absolute isolation from one another, if the artistic volition is at issue as the sole decisive factor. For the greatest difference between the two styles, namely the still distinct prevalence of the Antique heritage in Romanesque, is a factor which, from the point of view of artistic volition, can only be regarded as an impediment conditioned by external circumstances.

A consideration of Romanesque architecture shows us that the tendencies which were later to become supreme were already clearly foreshadowed there, even if still on the Antique fundament, which had not been lost either in Early Christian or Byzantine architecture. The Antique is present in Romanesque, as stated, not as a form clearly apprehended in its organic nature, but retained as an external scaffolding, as a firmly established type, with which the new artistic volition had perforce to come to terms. Only gradually did the architectonic ideas specific to the Northern artistic volition acquire strength.

In its inner constitution the Romanesque style already announces its Northern origins, as soon as we look beyond the Antique element in its nature, which adheres to it like something extraneous. Its overall attitude is abstract, and it bears somewhat the same relationship to Gothic as Doric does to the other Greek architectural styles. Like Doric, it too repudiates every impulse to empathy. We are confronted by a somewhat compressed, calm, serious architectural structure, in the details of which, however, the develop-

ment to come is already disclosed. The living tendencies are already contained in the system of flying
buttresses, in the rib-vaulting, and in the clusters of
pillars. That which is here trying to force itself through
on a foreign substratum later becomes the sole and
decisive factor. What was more likely than that these
tendencies, as they gradually grew stronger, should
have thrown off Antique decorum and created out of
themselves a new system in conformity with their own
artistic volition? Thus arose the Gothic style, which
gradually conquered the whole of North-west Europe.
We have already said that in the Gothic architectural
idea that indigenous artistic volition which we observed in ornamental art, and which we summarised
by the formula 'heightened expression on an inorganic
fundament', came to fulfilment and apotheosis. Faced
with a Gothic cathedral, the question of whether its
inner constitution is organic-living or abstract would
throw us into perplexity.—By inner constitution we
understand what may be described as the soul of a
building, the mysterious inner power of its nature.
Now the first thing we feel with the Gothic cathedral
is a strong appeal to our capacity for empathy, and
yet we shall hesitate to describe its inner constitution
as organic. This hesitation will be strengthened if
we think of the organic constitution of a Classical
Greek edifice. Here in the Classical edifice the concepts organic and empathy are completely co-extensive;
here an organic life is substituted for matter; it obeys
not only its own mechanical laws, but is subordinated,
along with its laws, to an artistic volition replete with
feeling for organic life. In the Gothic cathedral, on the
contrary, matter lives solely on its own mechanical
laws; but these laws, despite their fundamentally abstract character, have become living, i.e. they have

acquired expression. Man has transferred his capacity for empathy onto mechanical values. Now they are no longer a dead abstraction to him, but a living movement of forces. And only in this heightened movement of forces, which in their intensity of expression surpass all organic motion, was Northern man able to gratify his need for expression, which had been intensified to the point of pathos by inner disharmony. Gripped by the frenzy of these mechanical forces, that thrust out at all their terminations and aspire toward heaven in a mighty crescendo of orchestral music, he feels himself convulsively drawn aloft in blissful vertigo, raised high above himself into the infinite. How remote he is from the harmonious Greeks, for whom all happiness was to be sought in the balanced tranquillity of gentle organic movement, which is alien to all ecstasy.[16]

Gottfried Semper admirably felt out the uncanny element in this living mechanics and therefore termed the Gothic style scholasticism in stone. For scholasticism is likewise the climax of an effort to express an inner, living religious sensibility with abstract-schematic concepts, just as Gothic is the apotheosis of mechanical laws of construction, heightened in their expression by the capacity for empathy. It will be understood that this maximum exploitation of constructional possibilities to no other purpose than the attainment of an intensity of movement that surpassed organic life and swept the spectator away with it seemed to other peoples who, in consequence of their *température d'âme*, were closer to the Antique ideal, an absurdity, an uncanny barbaric extravagance.

We must return once more to a comparison with Greek architecture. There can be no doubt that it too is a purely constructional form, i.e. all its structures clearly proceed according to constructional laws. Now the tectonic of the Greeks consists in the animation of stone, i.e. an organic life is substituted for stone. That which is conditioned by the construction is subordinated to a higher organic idea, which takes possession of the whole from within outward and imparts to the laws of matter an organic illumination. We recall that this movement was already foreshadowed in the construction of the Doric temple, whose inner constitution is otherwise still purely abstract. In the Ionic temple and the architectural development ensuing upon it the purely constructional skeleton, which is based solely on the laws of matter, that is to say, upon the relationship between load and carrying power, etc., was guided over into the more friendly and agreeable life of the organic, and purely mechanical functions became organic in their effect. The criterion of the organic is always the harmonious, the balanced, the inwardly calm, into whose movement and rhythm we can without difficulty flow with the vital sensation of our own organisms. In absolute antithesis to the Greek idea of architecture we have, on the other hand, the Egyptian pyramid, which calls a halt to our empathy impulse and presents itself to us as a purely crystalline, abstract construct. A third possibility now confronts us in the Gothic cathedral, which indeed operates with abstract values, but nonetheless directs an extremely strong and forcible appeal to our capacity for empathy. Here, however, constructional relations are not illumined by a feeling for the organic, as is the process in Greek temple building, but purely mechanical relationships of forces are brought to view *per se*, and in addition these relationships of forces are intensified to the maximum in their tendency to movement and in their content by a power of empathy that extends to the abstract. It is not the life of an organism which we see

before us, but that of a mechanism. No organic harmony surrounds the feeling of reverence toward the
world, but an ever growing and self-intensifying restless
striving without deliverance sweeps the inwardly inharmonious psyche away with it into an extravagant
ecstasy, into a fervent excelsior. Was not Gothic, with
its morbid differentiation, with its extremes and with
its unrest, the age of puberty of European man?

Before leaving architecture we should like to contrast two characteristic quotations, one from Langier's
famous *Essai sur l'architecture* (1752) on Gothic, and
some words of Goethe's concerning the Antique.

Langier writes: 'La barbarie des siècles postérieures
fit naître un nouveau système d'architecture, où les
proportions ignorées, les ornaments bizarrement con-
figurés et puerilement entassés, n'offraient que des
pierres en découpure, de l'informe, du grotesque, de
l'excessif.'

And as the antithesis, Goethe's words concerning
the Antique: 'These lofty works of art were created,
at the same time, as the most elevated works of nature.
Everything arbitrary or fanciful falls away; there is
necessity, there is God.'

It is not surprising that as the Middle Ages advanced
architecture achieved sole sovereignty, and assigned a
secondary position to all other branches of art; for in
architecture the artistic volition characterised above
could be expressed with the least impediment. The
natural constructional preconditions of architecture
met half-way the tendency to render the abstract
expressive, and here no organic natural model opposed
itself to this volition.

In sculpture this artistic volition was bound to encounter a natural resistance. In as much, however, as
it did not renounce its aims in the face of this resist-

ance, but forced itself through notwithstanding, there arose those peculiar and strange figures of Romanesque and Gothic sculpture. In Romanesque sculpture we find the same state of affairs as in Romanesque architecture. Here the indigenous artistic volition is still experimenting on a fundament which is actually foreign to it, in this instance on the heritage of Graeco-Roman sculpture modelled in the round. Within this framework, however, the tendency to a low-relief style, and the tendency to give the line a life of its own, are everywhere in evidence, and they become stronger and stronger with the passage of time. The inherited swing of the Antique draperies becomes more and more rigid and more and more an ornament of linear abstraction in the manner of the hybrid formation of abstraction and expression delineated above. Drapery is already slowly becoming merely a substratum for these linear phantasies, already it is imperceptibly acquiring a separate existence *vis-à-vis* the body.[17] But despite all these individual factors, the Antique convention is still visible in compressed, somewhat flattened figures, e.g. of the Southern French Romanesque style. The tendencies which are here still expressed inconspicuously and on an alien fundament, shake off all decorum and restraint as they emerge in that development of monumental statuary upon whose threshold stand the sculptures of Chartres. The relatively calm proportions between verticals and horizontals which prevail in the Romanesque architecture and sculpture that is still guided by the Antique, are here conspicuously abandoned, and the human figure is drawn into the system of an inorganic heightened movement, just as in ornamental art and book illustration. It is not enough to designate the style of these unnaturally elongated, narrow figures subordination to the architectonic, for this does not cast sufficient light on the facts. It must rather be said that the same artistic volition was manifested in sculpture as in architecture; that simple sculptural reality did not suffice this artistic volition, because the expression afforded by this reality was not pathetic, not poignant enough, so that it sought to heighten the rendering of cubic reality into a more powerfully expressive abstraction. And it could find no more brilliant way of satisfying this aspiration than by causing the representation of figures to be drawn into the great maelstrom of those mechanical forces which, their movement intensified by the power of empathy, lived themselves out in architecture. Thus these columnar saints are a medium of expression, and with this expression they appeal to our capacity for empathy. The expression does not lie in the personal expressive value of the individual figure, however, but in the expressive abstraction that dominates the entire architectonic and upon which the statues, in their subordination to this architectonic, are entirely dependent. In themselves they are lifeless; it is only when they take their place in the whole that they participate in that intensified life which passes above and beyond everything organic.

In considering and evaluating medieval sculpture, account must be taken of a factor that is remote from our viewpoints, namely of that naturalism or realism, common to all Cis-Alpine art, which expresses itself in the typical. This realism is beyond the absolute artistic volition that is always based on the elementary aesthetic sensibilities alone and hence can be expressed only in formal terms. It pertains rather to a broader aesthetic that reckons with the boundless possibilities of the sensations of aesthetic complication. These sensations of complication appeal, above and beyond aesthetic experience, to the most diverse spheres of psychic experience; hence they are not susceptible of expression within the limits of the formal, and consequently, as already underlined in Chapter Two, are no longer accessible to aesthetics proper. They are individually determined and only individually apprehensible; thus they do not bear the character of necessity, with which alone a scientific aesthetic can reckon.

The typical then develops into the contentual in the widest sense, whose sphere of operation lies in quite different fields to that of pure aesthetic experience.

This realism had now to come to terms, in Romanesque and Gothic art, with the purely formal-abstract artistic volition. This led to an odd hybrid formation. The typifying imitation impulse seized upon the heads of the figures as the seat of expression of the soul; the drapery that suppressed all corporeality, however, remained the province of the abstract artistic urge.

The imitation impulse was also of great significance in so far as it threw a bridge over to the organic. Even though it proceeded provisionally in the direction of the typical and of the apprehension of verisimilitude, without arousing the feeling for the beauty of the organic, a factual basis was nevertheless thereby created, upon which it was possible for the feeling for the aesthetic-formal value of the organic to develop later, during the period of Antique and Italian influence.[18]

For the time being everything lay abruptly side by side; the realistic construction of the heads stood in abrupt contrast to the entirely abstract and inorganic conformation of the rest. To pursue from these viewpoints the evolution of Gothic sculpture would require a separate treatise. For in no other style do extremes and contradictions lie so close together. The disputation of two tendencies, so entirely disparate in principle, on so narrow a terrain was bound to lead to the sort of strange and imposing art that we find in Gothic sculpture. But how does this style dissolve into the art of the Renaissance? This process can, of course, only be hinted at within the framework of this essay.

We have already cited as the prime factor the disposition for the organic-formal tendencies from across the Alps which resulted from the urge to reproductive verisimilitude. With this we have taken only half a step however. The further evolution took place in an interesting process. We have already observed that the abstract tendencies of the Northern artistic volition rose to an apotheosis in the treatment of drapery. Drapery, with the phraseology of its ingeniously arranged folds, led an existence independent of the body; it became an organism on its own. Now a change also occurred within this Gothic phraseology. The important process of imparting an organic illumination to the inorganic now ran through the treatment of drapery. The way in which that rhythmic dominant we call Gothic line—which is really decisive only for the ponderation of the whole, but which, in its rhythm and in the verticalism of its proportions, still clung initially to the heightened and over-loud life of the previous epoch—worked its way out of the crinkled, angular, brittle drapery style of the early period; the way in which this Gothic line then slowly became calmer as it grew more organic and assumed an ever more rhythmic swing, until it attained perfect equipoise between horizontal and vertical tendencies; the way in which this rhythm, in a slow evolution, assimilated into itself the whole disorder of folds: all this can be followed only with the aid of illustrations. The process was complicated by the fact that, under the influence of the Italian Renaissance, the body also was now organised and rhythmicised, so that in the end body and drapery each sought to drown the sound of the other, like two separate orchestras, albeit both were playing in the same key. In that phase of the development of Gothic which we call Gothic Baroque, and whose representatives are mainly to be found in South Germany, the music of drapery drew together into a last full-toned symphony. Here it once more revelled in the most marvellous accords, which rang out far louder than the more modest and restrained rhythm of the body; but with this last effort it broke down, and the body emerged with ever greater clarity and autonomous sovereignty. The advanced understanding of the Renaissance then brought this dual operation of body and garments to a final end. The body became the dominant factor, the garments an epiphenomenon that compliantly subordinated itself to this dominant. The last echo of the Gothic drapery style had faded away, and with it the last reminiscence of the starting-point of Northern artistic creation, of that system of delineation which was at once abstract and expressive, was extinguished. Having worked its way, felicitously and along many detours, to organic lucidity, it had lost its *raison d'être* and was eliminated from the further course of evolution.

Therewith ends the long evolution that leads from the beginnings of linear ornament to the luxuriant turgescence of Late Gothic. The Renaissance, the great period of bourgeois naturalness, commences. All unnaturalness—the hallmark of all artistic creation determined by the urge to abstraction—disappears. With Gothic, the last 'style' goes under. Whoever has felt, in some degree, all that is contained in this unnaturalness, despite his joy at the new possibilities of felicity created by the Renaissance, will remain conscious, with deep regret, of all the great values hallowed by an immense tradition that were lost forever with this victory of the organic, of the natural.

Transcendence and Immanence in Art

ANY deeper enquiry into the nature of our scientific aesthetics must lead to the realisation that, measured against actual works of art, its applicability is extremely limited. This situation has long been evident in practice through the undisguised mutual antipathy that divides art historians and aestheticians. The objective science of art, and aesthetics, are now and will remain in the future incompatible disciplines. Set before the choice of abandoning the greater part of his material and contenting himself with a history of art cut *ad usum aesthetici*, or foregoing all the lofty flights of aesthetics, the art historian naturally opts for the latter, and the two disciplines, so closely related in their subject-matter, continue to pursue parallel paths devoid of any contact. Perhaps the sole cause of this misunderstanding is the superstitious belief in the verbal concept art. Caught up in this superstition, we again and again become entangled in the positively criminal endeavour to reduce the multiple significance of the phenomena to a single, unequivocal concept. We cannot shake ourselves free of this superstition. We remain the slaves of words, the slaves of concepts.

Whatever the cause may be, the position is in any

case that the sum of the facts of art is not co-extensive with the questions posed by aesthetics, but rather that the history of art and the dogmatics of art are incongruent, and even incommensurable, quantities.

If we were to agree to confine the term 'art' to those products answering the questions put by our scientific aesthetics, by far the greater proportion of the material hitherto appraised by art historical research would have to be rejected as not being art; there would remain only quite small complexes, viz. the artistic monuments of the various Classical epochs. Here lies the secret: Our aesthetics is nothing more than a psychology of the Classical feeling for art. No more and no less. No expansion of aesthetics goes beyond this boundary. To this the modern aesthetician will object that he long ago ceased to derive his principles from the Classical tradition, that he reaches them along the path of psychological experiment, and that nevertheless the results thus obtained find confirmation in Classical works of art. This merely implies that he is moving in a vicious circle. For in comparison with Gothic man, Ancient Oriental man, primeval American man and so forth, our contemporary humanity, despite all differentiation and higher organisation, shares the ground-lines of its psychic structure with the humanity of the Classical epochs; so that the whole contents of its culture is founded on this Classical tradition. Modern experimental psychology itself, with its investigation of the laws that govern aesthetic processes, is incapable of advancing beyond these ground-lines and rudimentary conditions of our psychic construction. In view of the manifest congruence between the intrinsically constitutive lines in the psychic structure of modern and Classical man, it is only to be expected that the most general results of modern aesthetics find confirmation in the material produced by Classical art, whereas, significantly enough the complicated development of modern art no longer fits exactly into this ABC-aesthetics. Thus the given paradigm of all aesthetics is and remains Classical art. This closely dependent relationship discloses, to whoever wishes to see, the whole problematic of our usual way of looking at the art of the past.

From this customary conception emanates a very simple schema of the evolution of art, which is orientated solely by the Classical zeniths. Thus the course of artistic evolution is reduced to an easily surveyed undulatory motion: that which precedes the Classical zeniths in question is regarded as an imperfect endeavour, but important as an indication of the heights to come; that which follows the zeniths is branded the outcome of decline and decadence. All our judgements of value move within this scale.

This mentally lazy and stereotyped assessment does violence to the real facts in a manner that cannot be allowed to pass without comment. For this way of looking at things from the narrow angle of our own era offends against the unwritten law of all historical research, that things must be evaluated not from our, but from their own presuppositions. Every stylistic phase represents, for the humanity that created it out of its psychic needs, the goal of its volition and hence the maximum degree of perfection. What seems to us to-day a strange and extreme distortion is not the fault of insufficient ability, but the consequence of differently directed volition. Its creators could *do* no otherwise because they *willed* no otherwise. This insight must precede all attempts at a psychology of style. For where there really exists a disparity between ability and volition in the productions of past epochs, it is obviously no longer perceptible from the great distance of our standpoint. The disparity that we believe we can discern, however, and that gives such a biased tinge to our judgements of value, is in truth only the disparity between our volition and the volition of the past epochs concerned; thus it is an entirely subjective antithesis, violently introduced into the tranquil, regular progress of events by our own bias. This is naturally not intended as a denial of the fact of development in art history, but merely to place it in the right light, in which it no longer appears as a development of ability, but as a development of volition.

The moment this illumination of the nature of artistic development strikes us, we see Classicism too under a new aspect. And we recognise the inner limitation which caused us to descry in the Classical epochs absolute zeniths and peaks of fulfilment of all artistic creation, although in reality they denote only particular and circumscribed phases of development, in which artistic volition was in *rapport* with the groundlines of our own volition. We therefore have no right to stamp the value which, under these circumstances, Classicism has for us, an absolute one; we have no right to subordinate to it the whole remaining complex of artistic creation. If we do so, we are caught up in an endless chain of injustices.

Only toward the Classical epochs can we be subjective and objective at the same time. For here this antithesis falls away, here we are guilty of no injustice if, with the lack of scruple common to all the rest of our art historical appraisal, we substitute our own volition for the ability of the past. But at the first step we take away from Classicism, whether backwards or forwards, the sin against the spirit of objectivity begins. We are certainly not capable of absolute objectivity, but this admission does not entitle us to stay at the commonplace viewpoint, instead of trying to reduce the measure of subjective short-sightedness and narrow-mindedness to a minimum. All the same, as soon as we leave the accustomed paths of our ideas, we find ourselves in trackless and unknown territory. There are no landmarks by which we can take our bearings. We have rather to create them for ourselves as we press circumspectly forward. Running the risk of taking our bearings not from theses, but from hypotheses.

No such difficulties faced us in the province of Classical art. Here we saw the ground-lines of our own volition realised in the ability of the past; once we pass beyond Classicism, however, this aid to comprehension is lost to us. Here we have rather to discover a new volition, with nothing to help us but mute, inert material. From the ability expressed in this material we have to deduce the volition underlying it. This is a deduction into the unknown, for which we have no guides *but* hypotheses. There is no possible means to knowledge here except divination, no certitude except intuition. But how poverty-stricken and menial would be all historical research without this great flight of historic divination. Or ought this kind of cognition to stand aside, when the other camp has nothing to offer but brutal violation of the facts by subjective bias?

Our knowledge of phenomena is complete only when it has reached that point at which everything which seemed to be a boundary becomes a transition, and we suddenly become aware of the relativity of the whole. To have known things means to have penetrated to the innermost nucleus of their being, where they disclose themselves to us in the whole of their problematic.

Similarly, we must first have grasped the phenomenon of Classical art in its most profound essence before we can recognise that Classicism does not constitute a finished and closed entity, but only a pole in the circling orbit of the artistic process. The evolutionary history of art is as spherical as the universe, and no pole exists that does not have its counter-pole. As long as our historical endeavours continue to revolve around the one pole which we call art, but which is in fact only Classical art, our vision will remain restricted and conscious only of the one goal. Only at the moment when we reach the pole itself do our eyes become opened, and we perceive the great beyond, that urges us toward the other pole. And the road that lies behind us seems suddenly small and insignificant in comparison with the infinitude that is now unfolded to our gaze.

The banal theories of imitation, which our aesthetics has never shaken off, thanks to the slavish dependence of the whole content of our culture upon Aristotelian concepts, have blinded us to the true psychic values which are the point of departure and the goal of all artistic creation. At best we speak of a metaphysic of the beautiful, leaving on one side everything unbeautiful, i.e. non-Classical. But alongside this metaphysic of the beautiful there is a higher metaphysic, which embraces art in the whole of its range and, pointing beyond all materialistic interpretation, finds its documentation in everything created, whether in the wood-carvings of the Maori or in any random Assyrian relief. This metaphysical conception is given with the knowledge that all artistic creation is nothing else than a continual registration of the great process of disputation, in which man and the outer world have been engaged, and will be engaged, from the dawn of creation till the end of time. Thus art is simply one more form for the expression of those psychic energies which, anchored in the same process, determine the phenomenon of religion and of changing world views.

One might just as well speak of Classical epochs of religion as of Classical epochs of art. Both are only variously modified manifestations of the Classical state of soul that has always existed when, in the great process of disputation between man and the outer world, that rare and fortunate state of equipoise has arisen in which man and world were fused into one. In the field of the history of religions, this state is marked by religions which start from the principle of immanence and which, wearing the various colours of polytheism, pantheism or monism, regard the divine as being contained in the world and identical with it. At bottom, indeed, this conception of divine immanence is nothing other than a total anthropomorphisation of the world. The unity of God and world is only another name for the unity of man and world. The parallel in the province of art history is not far to seek. The Classical feeling for art has its basis in the same fusion of man and world, the same consciousness of unity, which is expressed in humanity's attribution of a soul to all created things. Here too the presupposition is that human nature 'knows itself one with the world and therefore does not experience the objective external world as something alien, that comes toward the inner world of man from without, but recognises in it the answering counterpart to its own sensations' (Goethe). The process of anthropomorphisation here becomes a process of empathy, i.e. a transference of man's own organic vitality onto all objects of the phenomenal world.

The process of disputation between man and the outer world naturally takes place solely within man, and is in truth nothing else than a disputation between instinct and understanding. When we speak of the primitive condition of mankind, we all too easily confound it with the latter's ideal condition, and again and again dream, like Rousseau, of a lost Paradise of humanity in which all created things dwelt together in happy innocence and harmony. Yet this ideal condition has nothing to do with the primitive condition. The disputation between instinct and understanding, that attains a state of equilibrium only during the Classical epochs, began rather with an absolute preponderance of instinct over understanding, which only slowly took its orientation from experience in the course of spiritual evolution. The instinct of man, however, is not reverent devotion to the world, but fear of it. Not physical fear, but a fear that is of the spirit. A kind of spiritual agorophobia in the face of the motley disorder and caprice of the phenomenal world. It is the growing assurance and mobility of the understanding, which links the vague impressions and works them up into facts of experience, that first give men a conception of the world; prior to that he possesses only an eternally changing and uncertain visual image, which does not permit the emergence of a confident, pantheistic relationship to nature. He stands frightened and lost amidst the universe. Thus dependent upon the deceptive and ever-changing play of phenomena, that robs him of all assurance and all feeling of spiritual tranquillity, there grows in him a profound distrust of the glittering veil of Maya which conceals from him the true being of things. He is inhabited by a gloomy knowledge of the problematic nature and relativity of the phenomenal world. He is by instinct a critic of cognition. The feeling for the 'thing in itself', which man lost in the pride of his spiritual evolution and which has come to life again in our philosophy only as the ultimate result of scientific analysis, stands not only at the end, but also at the beginning of our spiritual culture. What was previously felt instinctively has finally become a product of thought. Here are the two poles between which the whole drama of spiritual evolution is enacted, a drama that seems great to us only so long as we do not watch it from these poles. For then the whole history of spiritual cognition and mastery of the world looks like a fruitless expenditure of energy, a senseless gyration. Then we succumb to the bitter compulsion to examine the other side of the process, which shows us how every advance of the spirit has rendered our picture of the world more superficial and more shallow, how it had to be paid for at each step by the degeneration of man's innate organ for the unfathomableness of things. It is immaterial whether we transport ourselves back to the starting-point, or set ourselves down at the end-point, which for us is Kant—from both points our European-Classical culture appears in the same highly questionable light.

For this culture of the physical world is confined to Europe and the countries with a European civilization. Only within these circles did human self-confidence dare to identify the true nature of things with the image which the spirit forms of them, and to assimilate all created things onto the human level. Only here was man able to fancy himself like God, for only here had he reduced the supra-human, abstract idea of the divine to a trite human notion. The Classical state of soul, in which instinct and understanding no longer represent irreconcilable opposites, but are fused together into an integral organ for the apprehension of the world, has narrower boundaries than our European arrogance admits.

The ancient cultural aristocracy of the Orient has

always looked down with superior contempt upon the European upstarts of the spirit. Their deep-rooted instinctive knowledge of the problematic nature of phenomena and the unfathomableness of existence prevent the emergence of a naïve belief in the values of the physical world. The outward knowledge of the Occident has also been conveyed to them, but it has found in their psychic constitution no anchorage to which it could make fast and become a productive element of culture. The real sphere of their culture remained unaffected by all intellectual cognition. The current which, in the Occident, bore the whole of cultural life, engendered in the Orient merely a fleeting ripple on the surface. Here no knowledge was able to stifle the consciousness of man's limitation and his helplessly lost situation in the universe. Here no knowledge was able to deaden his inborn anguish at the world. For this anguish did not stand, as with primitive man, *before* cognition, but *above* it. There is one great ultimate criterion for mankind's relation to the cosmos: its need of redemption. The form taken by this need is an unfailing guide to the qualitative variations in the psychic predispositions of individual peoples and races. Where religious notions assume a transcendental tinge, this is a sure sign of a strong need for redemption determined by the most profound world instinct. Accordingly, a slow dying down of the need for redemption runs parallel with the path from rigid transcendentalism to the conception of God as immanent. The network of causal connections between these phenomena is so clearly visible that it is sufficient to point it out. But, conversely, we are all the less familiar with the connections that exist between a state of soul which thus inclines toward transcendentalism, and the form of its expression in art. For the spirit's fear of the unknown and the unknowable not only created the first gods, it also created the first art. In other words: To transcendentalism of religion there always corresponds a transcendentalism of art, for which we lack the organ of understanding only because we obstinately insist upon appraising the vast mass of factual material in the whole field of art from the narrow angle of vision of our European-Classical conception. We perceive transcendental feeling in the content, to be sure; but we overlook it in the real core of the process of artistic creation, the activity of the form-determining will. For the idea that, under diverse presuppositions, art also represents a quite diverse psychic function, is remote from our biased European outlook.

Ultimately, all our definitions of art are definitions of Classical art. Greatly as they differ in detail, they all agree on the one point that all artistic production and enjoyment is accompanied by that state of inner psychic exaltation in which for us to-day artistic experience is localised. Without exception, they regard art as a luxury activity of the psyche, in which it discharges its surplus of vital energy. Whether it is the art of the Australian aborigines, or the art of the builders of the pyramids that is under discussion, the 'heaving breast' is taken for granted as a concomitant of art. It is true that for us the greater the calm and satisfaction with which our breast breathes, the more strongly we experience the sensation of beauty. Since for us the whole of art's capacity for bestowing happiness is comprised in the possibility it provides us of creating an ideal theatre for our inner experience, in which the forces of our organic vitality, transferred onto the work of art by means of empathy, are able to live themselves out uninhibitedly. For us, art is no more and no less than 'objectified self-enjoyment' (Lipps).

However, we must seek to emancipate ourselves from these preassumptions, which are to us axiomatic, if we wish to do justice to the phenomenon of non-Classical, i.e. transcendental art. Since to the art beyond Classicism artistic creation and experience represents the activity of a diametrically opposite psychic function which, remote from all reverent affirmation of the phenomenal world, seeks to create for itself a picture of things that shifts them far beyond the finiteness and conditionality of the living into a zone of the necessary and abstract. Inextricably drawn into the vicissitudes of ephemeral appearances, the soul knows here only *one* possibility of happiness, that of creating a world beyond appearance, an absolute, in which it may rest from the agony of the relative. Only where the deceptions of appearance and the efflorescent caprice of the organic have been silenced, does redemption wait. For the transcendental feeling toward the world the urge to master the things of the external world through art could never assume the expression of that Classical volition which believed it was gaining possession of things when it animated and transfigured them by its own human grace. For this would have meant nothing else than a glorification of that relation of interdependence between man and outer world, the consciousness of which had given rise precisely to the transcendental humour of the soul. For it, the only salvation lay rather in the greatest possible diminution and suppression of this agonising fact of dependence. To give things fixation in art could only mean to divest them of all but the minimum of their conditional mode of manifestation and of their inextricable entanglement with the external nexus of life, and in this way to redeem them from all the illusions of sensory perception.

Thus all transcendental art sets out with the aim of

de-organicising the organic, i.e. of translating the mutable and conditional into values of unconditional necessity. But such a necessity man is able to feel only in the great world beyond the living, in the world of the inorganic. This led him to rigid lines, to inert crystalline form. He translated everything living into the language of these imperishable and unconditional values. For these abstract forms, liberated from all finiteness, are the only ones, and the highest, in which man can find rest from the confusion of the world picture. These inter-relationships afford the decisive perspective for the authentic history of the evolution of that human expression of life which we call art. The great crisis in this evolution, which created a second and disparate empire of art, begins with the moment at which the understanding, breaking away from the matrix of instinct and trusting to itself, gradually took over that function of perpetuating perceptions which had hitherto been carried out by the activity of art. What happened was that translation into the laws governing the inorganic was brought to an end and replaced by translation into the laws governing the human spirit. Science emerged, and transcendental art lost ground. For the world picture set out by science and fashioned into a meaningful process, now offered the man who put his faith in the cognitive capacity of the understanding the same feeling of assurance that the transcendentally predisposed man had reached only along the laborious and joyless detour of complete de-organicisation and denial of life.

Only after this crisis did that latent force of the soul awake, in which our specific experiencing of art is rooted. It is an entirely new psychic function which now gradually masters existence in its own way. And only from this turning-point on can there be any question of what we call joy in art; for only now does the happy sensation of the 'heaving' bosom accompany all artistic activity. The old art had been a joyless impulse to self-preservation; now, after its transcendental volition had been taken over and calmed by the scientific striving after knowledge, the realm of art seceded from the realm of science. And the new art, which now springs to life, is Classical art. Its colouring is no longer joyless like the old. For it has become a luxury activity of the psyche, an activation of previously inhibited inner energies, freed from all compulsion and purpose, and the bestower of happiness. Its delight is no longer the rigid regularity of the abstract, but the mild harmony of organic being.

Here are the presuppositions in which the fundamental difference between the Oriental and the Occidental way of experiencing the world, between transcendental and Classical art, is anchored. Here is the problem from which all consideration of the art of the past must take its orientation, if it is to pass beyond a narrowly European outlook.

Notes

1. Cf. Hildebrand, *Problem der Form*: 'The problems of form which arise during the architectonic fashioning of a work of art are not those immediately posed by nature and self-evident, but precisely those which belong absolutely to art.' Or: 'The activity of plastic art takes possession of the object as something to be illumined by the mode of representation, not as something that is already poetic or significant in itself.' One must not be misled by the word 'architectonic'; as employed by Hildebrand it embraces all those elements which distinguish a work of art from mere imitation. Cf. the disquisition in the Preface to the Third Edition, in which Hildebrand formulates his artistic credo in lucid propositions.

2. This limitation is a dictate of necessity. For this cannot be the place to weigh against one another the various systems that proceed from the psychic process of empathy. We must therefore renounce any critique of Lipps' system here, especially as we are making use only of its basic general ideas. The development of the problem of empathy extends back to Romanticism which, with artistic intuition, anticipated the fundamental outlook of contemporary aesthetics. The problem received scientific elaboration at the hands of men like Lotze, Friedrich Vischer, Robert Vischer, Volkelt, Groos, and finally Lipps. Further information concerning this development is contained in the lucid and meritorious Munich dissertation by Paul Stern, *Einfühlung und Assoziation in der modernen Ästhetik*, Munich, 1897.

3. The ensuing attempt at a characterisation reproduces the fundamental ideas of Lipps' theory, in part verbatim, in the formulations given to them by Lipps himself in a summary of his doctrine which he published in January 1906 in the weekly periodical *Zukunft*.

4. My essay rests at various points on the views of Riegl, as set out in *Stilfragen* (1893) and *Spätrömische Kunstindustrie* (1901). A

136

knowledge of these works, if not absolutely necessary to the understanding of my essay, is at least highly desirable. Even if the author is not in agreement with Riegl over all points, he occupies the same ground as regards the method of investigation and it is to Riegl that the greatest incentives to the work are due.

5. Cf. Wölfflin in this connection: 'I am naturally far from denying a technological genesis of individual forms. The nature of the material, the method of working it, the construction will never be without influence. But what I wish to maintain—especially against certain new endeavours—is that technology never creates a style, but that where art is concerned a particular feeling for form is always the primary factor. The forms produced by technology must never contradict this feeling for form; they can endure only where they adapt themselves to this pre-existing taste in form' (*Renaissance und Barock*, II Aufl., 57).

6. One need only call to mind, for example, how bewildered even an artistically trained modern public is by such a phenomenon as Hodler, to name only one of a thousand instances. This bewilderment clearly reveals how very much we are accustomed to look upon beauty and truth to nature as a precondition of the artistically beautiful.

7. This is not intended to deny the fact that we are able to-day to empathise ourselves into the form of a pyramid, any more than the general possibilty of empathy into abstract forms, which we shall discuss at length in the ensuing pages. Only everything contradicts the assumption that this empathy impulse was at work in the creators of the pyramidal form. (See the practical section of the book.)

8. In this context we may recall the fear of space which is clearly manifested in Egyptian architecture. The builders sought by means of innumerable columns, devoid of any constructional function, to destroy the impression of free space and to give the helpless gaze assurance of support by means of these columns. (Cf. Riegl, *Spätrömische Kunstindustrie*, Chapter I.)

9. This problem will be dealt with in greater detail in Chapter Two.

10. Schopenhauer's aesthetic offers an analogon to such a conception. According to Schopenhauer the felicity of aesthetic contemplation consists precisely in the fact that in it man is delivered from his will and remains only as pure subject, as the pure mirror of the object. 'And precisely thereby, he who is

immersed in such contemplation ceases to be an individual, for the individual has lost himself in this contemplation: he is the pure, will-less, painless, timeless subject of cognition.' (Cf. Book Three of *The World as Will and Idea*.)

11. In his usual pellucid manner, so well adapted to the theme, Wölfflin has expressed this as follows: 'The Renaissance is the art of beautiful, tranquil being. It offers us that liberating beauty which we experience as a sensation of general well-being and a heightening of our vital force. In its perfect creations we find nothing oppressed or impeded, nothing restless and excited; every form has materialised freely and with absolute ease: the vaulting arches over in the purest circle, the relationships are broad and blithe, everything breathes satisfaction, and we believe it would be no mistake to discern in precisely this heavenly peace and freedom from exigencies the highest expression of the artistic spirit of that period' (*Renaissance und Barock*, II Aufl., 22f.).

12. As actually was attempted in the early period of the Roman Empire by the concept of the Pantheon; this passage constitutes one of the highpoints of Riegl's book. Here we get a full view of the grandeur of his interpretation, which, in spite of its intuitive character, adheres with all discretion and respect to scientific fact.

13. The whole of this plane theory, which will certainly strike anyone unprepared for it as somewhat bizarre and questionable, cannot be discussed in this context and in this framework at the length necessary to free it, as far as possible, from its dubious character. Since it rests upon Riegl's book, we may perhaps be permitted to refer the reader to the latter's sensitive and full exposition.

14. In his characterisation of Winckelmann, Goethe speaks of Antique natures. He understands by this 'an unfragmented nature which operates as a whole, knows itself one with the world and therefore does not experience the objective external world as something alien, which comes to meet the inner world of man, but recognises in it the answering counterparts to his own sensations'.

15. *Religion und Religionen*, Munich, 1906.

16. Compare Wölfflin on Gothic: 'All that the age contained of phantasy and extravagant exaggeration found expression in its architecture. Here something magnificent came into being. But it is a magnificence that lies beyond life, not life itself magnificently experienced' (*Die Kunst Albrecht Dürers*, 20).

17. The broken, angular style of drapery of this period has

been described as a legacy from wood-carving, where it was conditioned by the character of the material. We even doubt whether
the material character of wood is sufficient to explain such an
arbitrary and independent phenomenon; but we are still more
strongly opposed to the explanation, as simple as it is psychologically impossible and shallow, that a phenomenon of material
restraint such as this was carried over, without any understanding, to stone-carving and painting. There can be no doubt that
the roots of this phenomenon lie deeper.

18. Compare in this connection Wölfflin, who demonstrates
precisely by the individual instance of Dürer, 'how the slumber-
ing feeling for life of the North rose up into wakeful consciousness
on the fundament of Italian models'.

Index

INDEX